STUDIES IN ECONOMICS

Edited by Charles Carter
Vice-Chancellor, University of Lancaster

7

The Economics of Research and Technology

STUDIES IN ECONOMICS

G. L. S. Shackle Expectation, Enterprise and Profit
J. Wilczynski The Economics of Socialism
M. Capstick The Economics of Agriculture
A. P. McAnally Economics of the Distributive Trades
K. D. George Industrial Organization: Competition, Growth and Structural Change
A. B. Cramp Monetary Management

in preparation

R. C. Tress The Public Sector and the Private Sector
R. J. Ball Macroeconomic Planning
Hans Singer and Caroline Miles The Rich and the Poor Countries
J. G. Corina Wages and Earnings
Ian Bowen Demography and Economics
F. S. Brooman Money and Financial Institutions
G. A. Phillips and R. T. Maddock The Economic Development of Britain, 1918–1968
A. I. MacBean The Institutions of International Trade
R. D. C. Black The History of Economic Thought
Charles Kennedy The Distribution of the Product
Theo Cooper Economic Aspects of Social Security
Gavin McCrone Economic Integration
A. J. Brown Regional Economics
W. J. L. Ryan Demand
D. J. Horwell International Trade Theory
E. J. Misham Cost-Benefit Analysis

The Economics of Research and Technology

BY

KEITH NORRIS

Reader in Economics, Brunel University

AND

JOHN VAIZEY

Professor of Economics, Brunel University

London

GEORGE ALLEN & UNWIN LTD

RUSKIN HOUSE MUSEUM STREET

First published in 1973

ISBN 0 04 330227 0 hardback
ISBN 0 04 330228 9 paperback

⊂ C

Printed in Great Britain by
Alden & Mowbray Ltd
in 10 point Times Roman type
at the Alden Press, Oxford

PREFACE

This book has been chiefly written by Keith Norris, though we both planned it and wrote large parts of it together. The work is, however, mainly his.

We would like warmly to thank Charles Carter for his helpful comments and suggestions, and other colleagues at Brunel and elsewhere for advice and help. We are especially grateful to Keith Norris's secretary, Christine Stephens, for her hard and efficient work, and to Annemarie Maggs, Secretary of the Economics Department, for what she has done.

KEITH NORRIS
JOHN VAIZEY
Brunel University
Uxbridge
July 1972

CONTENTS

Introduction

None of the concepts in this book is simple. The whole notion of measuring economic welfare and the process of economic change is itself a very difficult one, because lying behind the numbers that are used is a whole series of judgements about the way life is lived and ought to be lived, which predetermine the values which are given to different parts of the economy. It is difficult to say without ambiguity that the world is a better place now than it was at a certain time in the past, and even more difficult to say that the way of life in China is better or worse than the way of life in Russia. That much is an economic commonplace, though it is surprising how often it is forgotten when judgements are made about the desirability or otherwise of economic growth.

But when we seek further to analyse the causes of economic growth, then indeed we enter the world of intangibles. Clearly, the most obvious difference between the world as it is now and what Peter Laslett has called the 'world we have lost', is the fact that there are many more people and things about than there used to be, and the connection between these things in all their abundance and the people who now live between two and three times as long as they used to live a hundred years or more ago is largely due to what we call *science*.

In the European languages there is no real word for science as we understand it. 'Science' corresponds to the whole of knowledge or systematic study, and is connected also with what we mean here by the word 'Arts', as in the phrase 'arts and sciences'—which is how most American undergraduate schools are referred to. In this book, we use 'science' in the Anglo-Saxon sense to mean primarily the natural sciences, and occasionally the social sciences; but it is important to remember the original sense of the word as the Europeans use it.

Clearly, the great growth in the amount of things which people have to use and work with has been connected with a fundamental change in the way that mankind knows the world. There has been a

11

profound change in the way that people understand the processes of the physical and biological world, and it is this change in the nature of human understanding which, embodied in technology and in human skills, has led to what we have called the process of economic growth, and the series of industrial revolutions through which mankind has lived since the mid-seventeenth century.

That much, then, also is almost a commonplace, yet to link in any systematic fashion the series of changes which have occurred in the past in the economy, and are occurring now with the changes in the organized body of knowledge, is a very complicated process of study and argument; and it is what this book is chiefly about. In order to present the argument carefully and simply, we have decided to set it out in skeleton form at this stage of the book.

In the first place, clearly, at some stage in the late Middle Ages, the processes of modern scientific thinking about the natural world began —probably just before or simultaneously with the rediscovery of Greek knowledge; and by the mid-seventeenth century it is fairly clear that the processes of scientific thought, mainly as we know them today, had become part of the wider humane understanding which formed the cultivated civilization of seventeenth-century Europe. During the eighteenth century, these processes of thought, and even more important, the cast of mind which was associated with the adoption of these processes, began to be applied on a widespread scale to the solution of ordinary human problems. It is widely recognized that a similar process occurred in China, but that scientific advance in China had not taken the form of modern Western European science which has now become 'world science'. It is also fairly clear that while this accumulation of scientific knowledge was associated with technological change, in the sense that people began to develop machines and to subdivide labour in the way that Adam Smith was to describe, the sheer level of technology was probably as high or even higher in parts of China than in many parts of Western Europe at the same time. That is to say, it would be too simple to argue from scientific discoveries to the process of technological change. Indeed, most historians would hold that the reverse was the case: it was the small series of technological changes which stimulated men to think in a scientific way, to pose for them problems for which they sought an answer. This is perhaps most strikingly true in the fields of mechanics and of elementary physics and chemistry, particularly with the series of experiments which were associated with the development of the steam-engine.

During the nineteenth century, scientific knowledge rapidly grew. It has been true, since about the turn of the eighteenth century, that most scientists at any point in time have been alive at that time because the number of scientists has been growing exponentially, generation by generation. It is also true, so far as these ideas can be given orders of magnitude, that the rate of innovation in new technologies steadily accelerated and that by the end of the nineteenth century the field of natural science had become a very specialized and detailed province which no one man could master, and that this series of scientific revolutions was associated fairly closely by that stage with a number of technological developments. The chief industry of which this was true was chemistry. In German universities there had been a great development of the science of chemistry which mirrored the technological advances in the chemical field that were occurring in Germany at the same time. There are many reasons why a great outburst of inventiveness in the field of chemistry might be regarded as one of the key phases of the revolution in many fields which occurred during the nineteenth century.

Most innovations in industry and commerce are small innovations and they are cumulative. Indeed it is only by looking backwards, as it were, that most innovations can be seen to be as significant as they have been. Yet this being said, there are nevertheless fundamental breakthroughs, either at the level of science or of technology, which transform the economic map. These, for example, include such things as the development of electricity, the introduction of oil, the invention of the aeroplane and, in our own time, the pharmaceutical revolution and the introduction of nuclear energy.

It is only in the twentieth century, and particularly since the First World War, that 'science based industries' as they are known, have become at all common. But they have now become so common that much of contemporary economic life could not exist if it were not for science. For example, the pharmaceutical industry, the synthetic-fibre industry, the rubber industry, the aviation industry, and much of the energy industry, all depend upon a knowledge of science which was largely absent before 1900, and a technology which is up-to-date in the strict sense.

Looking ahead, we therefore can see that society may very likely become increasingly science based, while it is already extensively science based, and that much of our present standard of living, good or bad as it may be, is dependent upon science and technology. We therefore have a series of questions to ask. The first is: what is the relationship between the amount of scientific activity at any point in time, and the advance of science? Would it be true, for example, to say that if you had one scientist you might make one breakthrough, while if you have ten scientists you might make ten breakthroughs? Or does the amount of science which is discovered diminish as the number of scientists increases? Secondly: does this pool of

13

knowledge, which is in essence an international pool freely available through the scientific journals, leak into technology? Or is technology subject to separate laws of its own? This then raises a further question: is technological advance dependent upon the amount of effort which goes directly into the process of technological innovation? Or is it largely a by-product of the growth of the economy and in particular of the growth of capital inputs? There is then the third major question: what is the relationship between the rate of growth of scientists and of science, and the rate of growth of technology and of technologists to the changes in the economy itself? That is to say, is the pattern a simple one of a scientific discovery, followed by technological innovation, followed, in turn, by its application to a particular economic problem, followed again by an accelerated rate of economic growth—or is the chain of causation the other way round, a particular economic problem, followed by a technological solution, followed by the scientific answer?

Now, clearly, problems posed as simply as this are not susceptible to simple answers, nor is it likely that any one set of answers, however qualified they may be, will apply to all economies at all times, or even to the whole of one economy at any one time. Nevertheless, a considerable amount of evidence now exists to enable a certain number of judgements to be made in this area. In a century-and-a-quarter, the number of universities in England has been multiplied by ten; in the world the growth of universities has been by one hundred. There are now over a hundred times more professors of physical science than there were a century ago in the U.K. Most school children study some science, and nearly half of them specialize in some degree in scientific subjects. It follows, then, that scientific knowledge has grown enormously and the amount of scientific research, measured by the time spent on it and the resources devoted to it, has increased by a factor of several hundreds over the past hundred years.

This is not the place to discuss the origins and nature of the scientific imagination and the series of revolutions which, cumulatively, have transformed man's view of the world and his place in it. But it is important to realize that, since 1860, when T. H. Huxley poured withering scorn on Bishop Wilberforce's sarcastic attack on Darwin, the great mass of the educated public has accepted science, and every educated person is to a greater or lesser degree aware of scientific principles. The many thousands of science graduates among the population are specialists in science; but we are all generalists in it.

This means that in our attitude to practical affairs we are likely to seek a scientific explanation of a problem. Though relatively few industrial, commercial, trade union, and political leaders are professional scientists, they are aware that science has a contribution to make. Inexorably and inevitably the scientific spirit has overtaken other attitudes, though it looks as if the tide might now be receding.

The next important fact is that, because of the great number of scientists, there is now a great number of scientific discoveries. Attempts have been made, none very satisfactory, to measure the importance of scientific discoveries. Perhaps the simplest is the number of scientific communications published, but on any scale some papers are more important than others. The general impression might be recorded that, though 'great discoveries' are still relatively rare, the tide of scientific knowledge is rising far more rapidly now than, say, fifty years ago. Newton compared a scientist to a boy picking up pebbles from a beach; the ocean was the measure of man's ignorance. Such imagery is apposite; but the impression is now rather of an excavator scooping up stones by the ton.

Two questions pose themselves for the economist. The first is: what economic limits are there to the process of 'pure' research? Secondly: what is the connection between this pure research, and innovation?

Research (as crudely defined above) is a function—perhaps a declining one—of the number of scientists. The number of scientists correlates very roughly with the size of higher education. 'Pure' research is what scientists do without direct technological aims in mind, though Pasteur's great discoveries came in work for a brewery, and, in turn, Madame Curie's work had direct therapeutic import-ance, so that the distinction between 'pure' and 'applied' science is a crude one. Attempts have been made to work out the 'pay-off' on research. They, too, are crude and unsatisfactory, since it is almost self-evident that scientific research (like art and museums) falls into that sector of human activity that is not undertaken directly for productive purposes, but to satisfy a deeply felt private and social concern. The resources to back that concern have steadily mounted as education has grown, though the high points of research funding have coincided with economic booms and urgent defence needs (as in the U.S.A. in the early 1960s), largely because it was assumed, though not proved, that research did have direct and immediate pay-offs in terms of economic growth and military strength. If anything, the relationship is the other way round, in the short run, or so it seems to us.

Yet, in the long run, there is clearly a connection between research and economic output. Modern medicine, for instance, rests almost entirely upon pharmacology which, in turn, rests on chemistry and biochemistry. Attempts have been made to estimate the relationship between scientific discoveries and their subsequent technological application. If anything, the time-lag, which in the cases so far considered averages about two generations, seems to be increasing. Such attempts at establishing connections of this sort have to be made as an essential part of the sociology of knowledge; but it is worth pointing out two handicaps in the research. The first is that many scientific 'discoveries' take the form of denying earlier discoveries. In our own discipline of economics, for example, Keynes's chief 'discovery' was the refutation of J. B. Say's law. Say's theory explained existing budgetary practice; it was eight years before Keynes's theory became accepted. Which was the 'discovery'? Secondly, most scientists are carrying out the same experiments as their colleagues in the same field. A great deal of scientific work consists of repeating other scientists' work. This is the essence of science, because it is not until something becomes well established by repeated experiments that a hypothesis takes on the air of virtual certainty. It follows, therefore, that much experimental work is not 'experimental' in the strict sense. One consequence of this is that it is difficult to say when a 'discovery' has occurred, and much anguish is caused by the desire to be first with a report in a scientific journal. Cases of multiple and simultaneous discovery are frequent; in economics, for instance, Keynes and Kalecki reached virtually the same conclusion simultaneously. This is hardly surprising. If several able and well trained people set about answering roughly the same question, they are likely to come up with the same answer. Science, therefore, is less an adventure into the unknown for many scientists, than a rationalization of their organized suspicion of all the others in the field.

An essential part of the game is its international character. There is no point in finding something out and hugging the secret to yourself—no Nobel Prizes are given for lights hidden under bushels, especially if the man next door is on to the same idea. As Watson tells us in his great book on the double helix, the wish to beat their rivals was often present in his and Crick's mind when they were unveiling the secret of life.[1] Scientists are just as likely to be vain, melodramatic men and women seeking recognition, no less than the rest of us.

The picture customarily given, then, of scientists making esoteric but essential discoveries for the common good, which can advance their country's interest well before that of some other country, is almost wholly implausible. Science is international because that is the essence of the way scientists work, and the result is that 'the pool of scientific knowledge' (to use a most inadequate metaphor) is open

[1] J. Watson, *The Double Helix*, Harmondsworth, Penguin, 1970.

for all who have a rod to fish in. It follows, therefore, t
a country need do no scientific research in order to
science: all it needs is a library that takes the leading
this is not wholly true. Since the work of most scientis
doing what other scientists are doing, it is only possibl
scientist to understand his field if he is well up in that fiel
less, it is true to say that there is little direct benefit in b
centre of scientific research; a few scientists keeping abr
coveries is (on this hypothesis) enough to enable a count
access to scientific knowledge and even, occasionally, to
ahead of the field—for nobody can be *well* ahead of the f
define 'field' as the dozen or so leading research groups in a
lar line of country.

And yet, however plausible this seems, there is an element
cynicism in this view. The application of science through tec
depends upon a widespread group of enthusiasts for scien
technology, well regarded, and in high places in commerce, in
and government. That such a group exists and is growing—c
growing until recently—marks one of the biggest differences be
the social environment now and a hundred years ago.

However, the great growth of science research and teaching-
the two are intimately connected—has not been due mainl
economic considerations. It has been largely a response to dema
for more education; and research scientists have themselves forn
powerful series of groups demanding additional funds from gove1
ment, business and charitable foundations. It is possible that a pe
son, in choosing a career, makes a calculation of his private di
counted rate of return as a research scientist compared with alterna
tives open to him. Some evidence suggests that this may be a plausible
explanation of some career choices. But it is certain that the allocation of total funds to research, and their division between different
branches of science, has not been done on this basis. It may be that
(in some views) they *ought* to be so allocated, to ensure a more
perfect allocation of resources; but so far they have not. As far as
can be seen, research allocations are largely made on grounds of
prestige in science and the 'promise' of various fields. Attempts to tie
these alternatives to the attainment of specified objectives have
usually met with failure.

Failure is perhaps inevitable, because two false models are implicit
in the assumption that an 'ideal' allocation of resources is possible.
The first assumes that what is unknown is in fact known. It cannot be
too strongly stressed that what is not known *is not known*. An
apparently obvious next step in research can be a step into the abyss
—as research into the common cold has shown! Much research

achievement is due to serendipity. And, secondly, it is not the case that a model such as 'problem→research→application' is either complete or customary. Often the application is discovered long before there is a problem. For instance, a tribe may feed itself on a balanced diet, and not realize that there is a nutritional problem until one ingredient becomes scarce. The tribe may remedy the deficiency by chance, or not remedy it at all. It follows, therefore, that any calculation as to what ought to be spent on research which is based upon the view that research will eventually find its way into application, as rain falls off the mountainside into the oceans, is based upon a misleading model. All knowledge is uncertain, and research is about ignorance. What is not known is what we are ignorant of; and the 'pool of knowledge', which is certainly available to all, is more like a pool in a fairy story, revealed only to those with special gifts, than a common-or-garden pond.

CHAPTER 1

Taxonomy

Our first task is to define clearly some of the terms which will crop up frequently in subsequent chapters. In this chapter is a series of definitions. We have deliberately spaced them out and we must emphasize that much of the value of economic analysis in this complex field depends upon clearing up a certain amount of terminological muddle. There are wide discrepancies between the use of the terms by economists and by scientists, technologists and others who are undertaking the activities which economists are discussing. Furthermore, there is no general agreement among economists as to standard definitions of terms, and there may well be disagreement among scientists and technologists, although this is not of immediate concern to us here. Inevitably a chapter of this sort tends to be rather dull, and we ask the reader to be patient.

We start by distinguishing between science and technology. 'Technology' is a good example of a word which is interpreted in several ways. We can identify at least five meanings in common usage:[1]

1. A general definition is that 'technology covers all the scientific and engineering activities in the process of industrial innovation'. This fails to distinguish between science and technology, a distinction which we shall wish to draw.
2. 'Technology can be taken as synonymous with engineering.' The basis of this interpretation seems to be that those who work in technology are usually trained engineers and have engineering qualifications.
3. Technology is often defined by engineers as a set of craft techniques. The practical emphasis inherent in this usage renders it similar to that suggested by Galbraith: 'The systematic application of scientific or other organized knowledge of practical tasks.'[2]

[1] See M. Fores, 'Some Terms in the Discussion of Technology and Innovation,' *Technology and Society*, 1970.
[2] K. Galbraith, *The New Industrial State*, London, Hamish Hamilton, 1967, p. 23.

19

4. There is the standard dictionary definition—'the science of the industrial arts'.

5. The meaning most commonly found in economics is a hybrid of the previous definitions. Technology is seen as defining a spectrum of available techniques, which define the various combinations of inputs which will yield any given (physical) output. Technology thus defines a production function.

No doubt there are many other interpretations of the word 'technology'. Enough has been said, however, to illustrate the nature of the problem. Although most interpretations have a certain similarity, there are enough differences to be a source of potential confusion. Each definition has its merits, but we have thought it worth while to set out at the start the precise meaning which we attach to various terms. We make no special claim for these—either in clarity or originality—and, in fact, in most cases we shall be simply restating a definition in fairly common usage. In any case, by drawing attention to the linguistic muddle, we have illustrated the protean nature of the matter we are dealing with. We will take *technology* to refer to the available set of techniques.

Science is the objective body of knowledge which has been accumulated and organized by systematic study. Thus, it is not confined to the understanding of natural or physical phenomena, and the characteristics which distinguish science from all other knowledge or understanding are that it must be objective and it must be possible to disprove it. Science is concerned with understanding, while technology is concerned with practicalities and with usefulness. Thus, technology is, in a sense, the embodiment of science in a set of techniques.

At various points in the book we shall examine the relationship between science and technology, but it should be emphasized at this point that the links between the two are not simple and are far from being perfectly understood. In some cases an addition to scientific knowledge is seen to lead directly to a change in technology. This was true of the development of nylon which was undertaken by E. I. du Pont de Nemours & Co. in the U.S.A. between 1927 and 1938. The company decided, in 1927, to allocate $250,000 annually to a programme of basic research into polymerization. The work was undertaken by a young chemist named Dr Carothers. In the next three years, the work can be said to have led to an advance in the scientific knowledge of the process by which molecules join together to form polyesters. In 1930 it was noticed during an experiment that as the heated polymer was withdrawn from a vessel, it could be drawn out in the form of a fibre and that the fibre remained tensile even

20

when cold. However, it was easily softened by heat. This phenomenon had not been observed before. It was thought that some similar polymer could be developed which would form a fibre for use in textile manufacture. Later work resulted, in 1938, in the construction of the first pilot plant to produce nylon. At this point a change in technology occurred.[1]

To be able to identify a clear causal link between a change in technology and some previous change in science is the exception rather than the rule. A recent study of eighty-four technological advances could only identify two cases where the route could clearly be traced back to scientific research.[2] It seems that most technological advances are based simply upon previous technological knowledge. This has been true of some very striking advances. For example, Dr Christiaan Barnard has written: 'In performing the first heart transplant I operated as a technologist. The only scientist involved was William Harvey, the man who gave us an understanding of the nature of the heart back in 1628. In much the same way I suspect that Isaac Newton was the only real scientist involved in putting man on the moon.'[3] It is also self-evident that many results of scientific research by their nature do not lead—and are not intended to lead—to any change in the productive processes or to new products. In Chapter 8 we further examine this complex and interesting question.

Research is the process of adding to the total, or advancing the limits, of scientific knowledge. It is customary to distinguish between *basic*, or *pure*, research and *applied* research. The former is undertaken with no specific commercial objectives, while applied research tackles problems with immediate commercial potential. Again, the distinction is often vague. Some basic research is undertaken in the laboratories of firms and it is difficult to see why they should incur such expenditure if there were no prospect of monetary return. Thus, it is important to emphasize that, while basic research has no specific or immediate commercial objectives, it clearly may have commercial potential. Firms, of course, have many objectives and survival is more important for some than profit maximization; others may undertake research because they want to, not because it helps them. But over the whole range of firms commercial principles probably

[1] A more detailed account is given as a case history in: J. Jewkes, D. Sawers and R. Stillerman, *The Sources of Invention* (2nd edn), London, Macmillan, 1969, pp. 275–77. This invaluable book should be studied carefully for the light it throws on the topics discussed here and subsequently, as well as for its general interest and importance.

[2] J. Langrish *et al.*, *Wealth from Knowledge*, London, Macmillan, 1972.

[3] C. Barnard, *Heart Attack*, London, W. H. Allen, 1972, p. 163.

predominate. Most research is, as we shall see, undertaken in the public sector, at least in the U.K.

Commercial objectives become paramount in the *development* stage of a new process or product. Development can be seen as the process of selecting the most (commercially) promising research results and using them to create new products or processes. The development phase includes the construction of prototypes or pilot plants. Throughout the development phase economic constraints operate. Only processes or products that are likely to be profitable in given market conditions will be ultimately used, and hence development is concerned with identifying these processes and discarding others. An integral part of development activity is *design* and it is here above all that commercial and production possibilities are exhaustively considered. The end of the development phase occurs when a new process is introduced into production, or when a production line is set up to produce a new product or to exploit a new process. Where do invention and innovation fit into this?

Invention is the creation of new technological knowledge; an *innovation* is the embodiment of this knowledge in actual productive processes. Thus, it is invention that changes the set of techniques available, while innovation changes the technology. It is not until innovation occurs that an invention has an effect on the way goods are produced, or on the type of product. In the past the distinction between invention and innovation was often easy to make in practice, for the inventor and the innovator were different people or organizations. The inventor sold the rights of his new technique (or product) to a firm who subsequently applied it in production. Today, although it is easy to underestimate the role of the individual inventor, invention and innovation often take place within the same organization, which tends to blur the distinction between them.

The main point at issue is whether an invention makes use of available and existing scientific knowledge, or whether invention may include some element of scientific discovery. It is argued, for several important reasons, that the distinction between invention and discovery is worth making.[1] First, scientific discovery is not concerned with usefulness or practicality, and indeed most discoveries are not immediately useful. Secondly, a scientist is now a recognized professional worker, in a university or research laboratory, publishing his results for scientific purposes. An inventor is a different animal, usually concerned with patenting his results, and often (as many studies have shown) an 'odd bird'. A scientist may

[1] S. Kuznets, 'Inventive Activity: Problems of Definition and Measurement', in: National Bureau Committee for Economic Research, *The Rate and Direction of Inventive Activity*, Princeton, Princeton University Press, 1962.

22

be an inventor, but the two functions are distinct. Finally, scientific discovery is general in the sense that it may provide the base for a large number of inventions. There is, in fact, usually a long time lag between discovery and invention, especially at periods when the advance of scientific knowledge is rapid. Science is international and simultaneous discoveries are frequent. This was brought out clearly in the discovery of DNA. Had Watson and Crick not cracked the secret, then Pauling in the U.S.A. would shortly have done so.[1] Because of the generality of discovery and because of the time-lags, the possibility of the patentability of a change may make the distinction clearer: inventions are patentable, discoveries are (usually) not. On this criterion, invention occurs subsequent to—or at least separate from—research, which we have defined as the process of adding to scientific knowledge. This conceptual distinction may, of course, be rather difficult to draw in practice, but it is a very important one, as we hope to show.

Having separated invention from research, only part of the problem of distinguishing the terms from each other has been solved. We can either place invention at the culmination of applied research activity or we can place it in the development phase. Many inventions in a patentable form occur in the development phase, yet development is often defined as the improvement of inventions. We have taken invention to be the creation of a new technique. An invention may follow some research findings, but it has usually arisen in the process of developing some other process.

An example of such an invention is the float-glass process, by which liquid glass is drawn on to molten tin. The bottom surface takes on the mirror-finish of the molten tin, while heat applied from above eliminates imperfections on the upper surface. The concept of using molten tin was first patented in 1902, but the float-glass process was not patented until 1959, by Pilkingtons, following seven years of intensive development work.

It is easier to place innovation in the research and development process. It occurs at the end of the development phase when a new process is introduced into production or when a productive line is set up to produce a new product. At this point the economic impact is immediate; Pilkington's float-glass process is an example. There is the problem, however, that improvements to processes and products occur subsequently to innovation. Many weaknesses become apparent only when production takes place on a significant scale. Thus, some development will take place subsequently to innovation and this may be initiated and partly undertaken by production

---

[1] J. Watson, *op. cit.*

personnel. This serves to emphasize, once more, the overlap of research, development and production.

We finally need to distinguish between *technological change* (or *advance*), a *change in technique* and *technical progress*. A *technological change* is a change in the available set of craft techniques, whereas a *change in technique* occurs when there is a change in the technique(s) chosen out of the available spectrum of techniques. Such a change may occur in response to a change in factor supply or price. In the simplest case the technology may offer various ways, some using a lot of labour, some using many capital goods, of producing some commodity. In ordinary economic reasoning it is held that, if wages rise relative to the price of capital goods, then firms may tend to select a more capital intensive technique in order to reduce their production costs.

This distinction is conceptually neat, but in practice it is very difficult to make because technological change occurs at the same time as relative factor prices change. We can, however, make the distinction in some cases. The first automatic cotton picker was produced in 1924, adding a new technique to those available. The automatic cotton picker saves labour, and in the late 1920s and early 1930s the massive unemployment in the U.S.A. meant that the optimal technique for cotton picking remained the traditional method of picking cotton by hand. By the end of the Second World War, conditions had changed and the cotton picker began to be produced—and used—on a commercial scale. Even in this case it is not totally realistic to separate out changes in technology from changes in the technique used, for the employment situation led to the Harvester Co. postponing its efforts to improve the rather inefficient cotton-picker it had first produced in 1924.

So what does the term 'technical progress' mean? Here it is very important to make clear that the term as used in most of the literature, and as we shall use it, does not necessarily have anything to do with science and technology. To be more specific, 'technical progress' should not be confused with the terms 'technological change' (or 'advance') and 'changes in technique'. Let us first be precise about technical progress. It is convenient here to talk in terms of an aggregate production function—we need not worry at this point about the problems associated with the use of such functions.

If we write an aggregate production function

$$X = F(Q_1, Q_2 \ldots Q_n)$$

where X is a vector of output, Q_1 is the amount of input 1, etc., then, given a time-series of inputs we can (assuming the form of the production function to be constant) predict the output of the economy

24

in question. It appears that when this is done the actual output is often greater than the predicted output. The unexplained difference, or residual, is said to be a measure of technical progress. Some of this technical progress will be due to scientific and technological influences, but some will be due to a multitude of other influences. For example, shifts of factors from low productivity sectors to high productivity sectors, or improvement in the average level of skill possessed by the labour force. Thus, the term *technical progress* is a 'catch-all'. Any changes in national output that cannot be explained by increases in inputs are termed 'technical progress'. Due to conceptual and statistical problems in measuring the inputs in a production function, much technical progress will be purely statistical, arising from measurement errors.

Part of the growth of output per head is due, directly or indirectly, to scientific and technological advance. A conclusion of this book is that most growth influences are complementary. This is particularly true of the exploitation of technological advances which often require changes in customer attitudes and in supplier industries. In addition, it will necessitate the acquisition of new skills by workers, and advances will have to be embodied in new plant and machinery. Technological advance has tended to be concentrated in the fastest-growing sectors (at least of manufacturing industry), and in sectors (e.g. computers, complex electronic systems and petrochemicals) where there are economies of scale. It is difficult to estimate the contribution made by science to economic and social development as simultaneous changes have occurred, although many of these changes have themselves been stimulated by scientific and technological change. These points will be discussed at some length in Chapter 11.

CHAPTER 2

Resources Devoted to Science and Technology

INTRODUCTION

The borders between activities that are directed towards adding to the stock of scientific and technical knowledge and activities which have other aims is notoriously vague. In industrial firms, for example, improvements to line processes are often made by production staff yet are more properly considered as a technological change. In universities, most staff undertake both teaching and research. We have to make a distinction between these various activities if we are to proceed, but it should be constantly remembered that the distinction may not always be clear-cut and may in some cases be an artificial one. The corollary to this, of course, is that statistics measuring the scale of resources devoted to science and technology are open to similar objections and should be interpreted with some caution. We first examine indications of the scale of these activities and attempt to give some idea of their rate of growth.

Three indications of the size of the 'science and technology industry' are used, two of which refer to inputs and one to outputs. The two measures of inputs are expenditure on research and development and the employment of qualified scientists and engineers, while the number of patents issued give one indication of the output arising from these inputs.

EXPENDITURE ON RESEARCH AND DEVELOPMENT

In 1967/8,[1] the latest year for which complete figures are available, expenditure on research and development in the U.K. was £962 million, or 2·8% of the Gross Domestic Product (GDP) at factor cost. Unfortunately, it is not possible to obtain reliable estimates for total research and development expenditure for years earlier than 1955.

There is no obvious price deflator to apply to the expenditure in current prices, but it can be seen from the right-hand column in

[1] Hereafter, financial years will simply be denoted by the most appropriate calendar year: thus, 1967/8 will be written as 1967.

TABLE 2.1. *Expenditure on Research and Development: U.K.*

	Expenditure on Research and Development (£m at Current Prices)	Research and Development as proportion of GDP at Factor Cost (%)
1955	300	1·9
1961	658	2·7
1964	771	2·7
1967	962	2·8

Sources: *Statistics of Science and Technology, 1970*, London, HMSO, 1971.
Annual Report of the Advisory Council on Scientific Policy 1956–1957, London, 1957.
National Income and Expenditure, 1970, London, HMSO, 1971.

Table 2.1 that since 1961 this expenditure has grown at roughly the same rate as has the GDP. It is not possible to say whether this has also been true of real expenditures, but it does not seem likely that the prices of research and development inputs have increased at such a different rate from all prices to upset the general conclusion. The 1955 estimate comes from a different source and it is possible that it may be a slight underestimate. From other evidence, however, there seems little doubt that there was a relatively rapid expansion

TABLE 2.2. *Relative Expenditures on Research and Development, 1963*

(U.S.A. = 1,000)

Austria	1
Belgium	6
Canada	20
France	62
Germany	68
Greece	(0·4)
Ireland	(0·5)
Italy	14
Japan	42
The Netherlands	16
Norway	2
Portugal	(0·5)
Spain	1
Sweden	12
Turkey	1
U.K.	103

Source: *A Study of Resources Devoted to R & D in OECD Member Countries in 1963/4*, vol. II, Paris, OECD, 1968, pp. 36–7.

of research and development expenditure in the 1950s and also in the period 1930–50. From this rather fragmentary evidence and from estimates for the U.S.A., it seems that at some stage of economic development such expenditures claim an increasing share of a country's resources followed by a levelling out. A similar conclusion emerges from an inter-country analysis of research and development expenditures, but before looking at this, we give some general indication of the scale of the research and development effort in OECD countries.

We must emphasize that these comparisons are subject to all the usual caveats made when making international comparisons.[1] In this case there is the additional difficulty that it is hard to be precise as to which expenditures are properly classified as 'research and development'. We have already pointed this out when making observations within one country, and the difficulties are compounded when we are looking at data for different countries. It therefore seems correct to draw only broad conclusions from the figures.

If we look at the absolute scale of research efforts, the most striking fact is the extent to which the size of the expenditure of the U.S.A. on research and development dwarfs that of any other country. Its expenditure is, for example, three times as great as that of all Western European countries combined.

The U.S.A. spends ten times as much on research and development as does the U.K., which has the largest research and development effort in Western Europe. These comparisons are based on converting expenditures to a common currency, using official exchange rates. It has been argued that official exchange rates do not reflect at all accurately the comparative cost of the resources—especially highly trained manpower—used in research and development. For example, Freeman calculated that in 1962 when the official exchange rate was £1 = \$2.80, a reasonable 'research exchange rate' would have been £1 = \$5.00.[2] Freeman has calculated research exchange rates for six of the countries listed in Table 2.2, and the comparative expenditure figures when these exchange rates are used are shown in Table 2.3.

The effect is more or less to double (relative to the U.S.A.) the expenditure of each of the five European countries. So, although the use of research exchange rates narrows the difference, the dominance of the U.S.A. remains.

[1] For a discussion of these problems and an attempt to evaluate educational expenditures on a consistent basis, see: J. Vaizey et al., The Economics of Educational Costing: Vol. I, Lisbon, Gulbenkian Foundation, 1969.

[2] C. Freeman and A. Young, The Research and Development Effort in Western Europe, North America, and the Soviet Union, Paris, OECD, 1965.

TABLE 2.3. *Comparisons of Research and Development Expenditures, 1963*

	Gross National Expenditure on R & D: Converted at Official Exchange Rates	Gross National Expenditure on R & D: Converted at 'Freeman' 1962 Exchange Rates
U.S.A.	1,000	1,000
Belgium	6	12
France	62	97
Germany	68	121
The Netherlands	16	30
U.K.	103	191

Source: See Table 2.2 Source, pp. 31, 36–7.

We now turn to the proportion of Gross National Product (GNP) devoted to research and development. The U.S.A. devotes the highest proportion of its GNP to research and development expenditure, followed by the U.K. and a group of advanced Western European countries which devote over 1·5% of their GNP to research and development. The lowest spenders (proportionately to GNP) are the less developed nations in the group, namely, Greece, Portugal and Spain. This suggests that there is a positive association between *per capita* GNP and the proportion of GNP allocated to research expenditures. There is a correlation of 0·81 between these two variables. Let us note the fact, however, that countries with similar *per capita* incomes spend considerably different proportions of their GNP on research and development. For example, The Netherlands spends three times more than Norway, and Belgium spends as high a proportion as Canada which is a much richer nation.

The picture is complicated further when we consider only 'economically motivated' research and development. In Table 2.4, economically motivated research and development is taken to comprise research and development expenditures (irrespective of the source of finance) undertaken in manufacturing industry, construction, transportation, telecommunications, and agriculture. This is a rather arbitrary definition as it will include some aerospace expenditures undertaken for strategic or prestigious reasons. The proportion of research and development expenditures that fall into the category is seen to vary widely between countries, being particularly low in the U.S.A. When economically motivated research and development expenditure alone is considered, the U.S.A. ceases to spend, proportionately to national income, more than any other country. The

TABLE 2.4. *Research and Development Expenditures and Gross National Product, 1963*

	(1) GNP *per capita* at Factor Cost	(2) R & D Expenditure as percentage of GNP at Factor Cost	(3) Proportion of R & D Expenditure that was Economically Motivated (%)	(4) Economically Motivated R & D as percentage of GNP at Factor Cost
Austria	1,021	0·3	62	0·2
Belgium	1,330	1·1	82	0·9
Canada	1,855	1·2	51	0·6
France	1,422	1·9	41	0·8
Germany*	1,538	1·6	62	1·0
Greece*	513	0·2	61	0·1
Ireland	704	0·5	89	0·4
Italy	845	0·7	63	0·4
Japan	633	1·5	73	1·1
The Netherlands*	1,286	2·1	70	1·5
Norway	1,386	0·8	56	0·4
Portugal*	333	0·2	72	0·1
Spain*	525	0·2	64	0·1
Sweden*	2,038	1·6	50	0·8
Turkey*	222	0·4	n.a.	n.a.
U.K.*	1,526	2·6	51	1·3
U.S.A.	3,058	3·6	28	1·0

Source: See Table 2.2 Source, vol. I, p. 58; vol. II, pp. 36–7.
* 1964.

tendency of the high-income countries to spend proportionately more on 'non-economic' research and development means that there is a weaker relationship between income *per capita* and the proportion of national income devoted to economically motivated research and development; here the coefficient of correlation falls to 0·56.

In summary, the U.K. is a relatively large spender on research and development, both in absolute terms and in proportion to national income. Expenditure in the U.K. has been increasing in line (roughly) with national income, since 1961, and probably faster than national income in the period 1930–61. Experience in the U.S.A. has probably been similar, although the reduction in the rate of growth seems to have occurred earlier. The scale of the research and development effort in the U.S.A.—as measured by expenditure—is greater than that of any other Western country. The dominance of the U.S.A. is much reduced when only economically motivated expenditure is included and when comparisons are made using research exchange rates. For example, from the crude overall figures (Table 2.2), expenditure in the U.K. in 1963 was 10% of that in the U.S.A. When both adjustments are made this proportion would seem to increase to around 33%. Finally, there is some tendency for richer countries to devote a higher proportion of their resources to research and development, although this relationship is not very strong when economically motivated expenditures only are considered.

<h3 style="text-align:center">QUALIFIED SCIENTISTS AND ENGINEERS</h3>

The stock of qualified scientists and engineers is another indicator of the resources devoted to science and technology. To some extent it is complementary to figures of research and development expenditure, as normally about one-half of such expenditure is devoted to salaries and wages. On the other hand, not all qualified scientists and engineers are employed on research and development (in 1968 in the U.K. the proportion was 31·5%), and therefore the manpower figures give a broader picture. This is important, since a conclusion that emerges from our later analysis is that it is essential—in order to take the fullest advantages of advances in science and technology—to have qualified, scientific manpower in production, sales, marketing, and in management generally. Of course, it is possible to extend this line of reasoning further to include people holding some educational qualifications in any subject. For a complete understanding of the process of innovation and the diffusion of innovation, this may well be necessary, and thus a discussion of the growth of education would be relevant. We shall restrict ourselves, here, to examining the growth of the stock of qualified scientists and engineers (see Table 2.5). The

TABLE 2.5. *Number of Qualified Scientists and Engineers:*
*U.K.**

	Nos. (1,000s)	Rates of Growth (% per annum)
1956	142	—
1965	211	4·5
1968	240	4·4
1971	279	5·1

Sources: *Statistics of Science and Technology*, London, HMSO, 1970, p. 115.

G. Payne, *Britain's Scientific and Technological Manpower*, London, Stanford University Press, 1960, p. 29.

* Refers to holders of a first degree or equivalent qualification in engineering, science or technology.

stock of qualified scientists and engineers has thus increased faster than expenditure on research and development and faster than GNP. Given the tendency over this period for educational expenditure to account for an increasing proportion of national income this is not an unexpected result. It is known that the proportion of qualified scientists and engineers employed in research and development

TABLE 2.6. *Indicators of the Relative Size of Research*
and Development Efforts, 1963

	Gross National Expenditure on R & D	Qualified Scientists and Engineers Employed on R & D
U.S.A.	1,000	1,000
Austria	1	4
Belgium	6	12
Canada	20	29
France	62	69
Germany	68	71
Greece	(0·4)	2
Ireland	(0·5)	2
Italy	14	41
Japan	42	245
The Netherlands	16	20
Norway	2	5
Portugal	(0·5)	2
Spain	1	9
Sweden	12	35
Turkey	1	—
U.K.	103	127

Source: See Table 2.2 Source, vol. II, pp. 36–7.

declined between 1965 and 1968, but it is not clear whether this is true of the whole period.

The numbers of qualified scientists and engineers can be used also to make comparisons between countries. It is difficult to find a common criterion for what constitutes a 'qualified' scientist or engineer, but it is interesting that the use of numbers of qualified scientists and engineers gives a slightly different picture from the use of research and development expenditures (see Table 2.6). In every case the disparity of the major industrial countries with the U.S.A. is reduced and, although the rankings are much the same in each case, there is one significant change: Japan ranks fifth on the basis of expenditure, but moves to second place when the alternative criterion is used. The reduction in difference in research and development effort when numbers of qualified scientists and engineers are used, could be due to the false picture given by official exchange rates, or it could mean that each qualified scientist or engineer had more resources to work with in the U.S.A. We can shed some light on which is the case by referring back to Table 2.3. It is clear, at least for the five countries for which data is available, that the difference in the comparisons is due largely to the use of official, rather than research, exchange rates.

PATENT STATISTICS

Both of the above measures are of resources used in science and technology. Patent statistics provide one measure of the output gained from these resources. It is not the only measure of output available—one alternative is to use the number of articles in scientific and technical journals—but it is the only measure that reflects the scale of inventive activity.[1] Thus, it is a measure—albeit an imperfect one—of the economic output of research and development. Many of the results of research and development will not be reflected in patent statistics. Most research results are, by definition, not patentable. The British patents laws, for example, specifically exclude theoretical ideas and scientific principles. Similarly, many of the activities that are classified as development will not result in a patent application. So patent statistics are, at best, a very partial measure of the output of scientific and technological activities. They are, however, the only direct measure we have, and there is the added advantage that patent statistics are available, for the U.K., for long periods of time. There are, unfortunately, several breaks in the series and it seems wisest to pay most attention to the years subsequent to 1950.

[1] For any analysis of the growth of science based on scientific publications, see: D. de Solla Price, *Little Science, Big Science*, New York, Columbia University Press, 1963.

In order to use data on patent applications (or data on patents granted) as a measure of inventive activity, one has to make two assumptions. First, that the ratio of patents to inventions remains constant over time. There are two main forces, apart from changes in legislation, which might make for a change in this ratio. Firms—most patents are taken out by firms—may come to rely, to a greater or lesser extent, on secrecy as an alternative method of protecting their inventions and, secondly, the standards of patentability applied by the patent office may have changed. It is usually agreed that, if anything, standards have become more severe, and it has been suggested that Edison's application for a patent on his incandescent-bulb would not be granted today. The second assumption that has to be made is that the 'average' invention in any year must be of equal 'importance' to the average invention in all other years. The problem is that when using statistics of patents, every patent—and therefore the associated invention—is given an equal weight. Thus,

TABLE 2.7. *Patent Applications: U.K., 1950–70*

	Number	Average Annual Percentage Rates of Growth over each 5-year Period
1950	31,686	—
1955	37,551	3·5
1960	44,914	3·6
1965	55,507	4·3
1970	62,101	2·3

Source: *Annual Reports of the Comptroller General of Patents, Designs, and Trade Marks.*

the patent on xerography is counted as being equal to a patent on a child's toy. To be more precise, we have to assume that the distribution of patents by importance is unchanged from year to year. There is little evidence on the validity of either of these assumptions, but there are clearly reasons for being cautious in the conclusions we draw from this data.

The most reliable series on patents seems to be that for patent applications (see Table 2.7). The principal alternative, the figure of patents sealed, exhibits marked, year-to-year fluctuations, which limits its usefulness for our present purposes.

About 90% of patents relate to manufacturing industry, and over the whole period 1950–70 the rate of growth of patent applications is the same as the rate of growth of manufacturing output at constant prices. This confirms the suggestion that inventive activity reflects the overall level of economic activity, although the relationship is by no means a close one in individual years.

CONCLUSION

The amount of resources directly devoted to science and technology in the U.K. is quite substantial. Expenditures on research and development accounted, in 1968, for 2·8% of GDP and the number of qualified scientists and engineers was 1·2% of total employment.

The U.K. ranks second or third (according to the criterion used) in this respect to the U.S.A. among the Western industrial countries.

How this money is spent and how this qualified manpower is deployed, and the reward from this effort, will be the subject of most of the rest of this book.

CHAPTER 3

Individual Inventors and Patents

In this chapter we consider the individual inventor. We also find it convenient here to discuss the patent system, although this is clearly relevant as well to our discussion of industrial research and development activities. The first question we seek to answer is whether invention depends upon individual inventors, in the sense that the aim of a policy to maximize invention should be to liberate individual inventiveness. This is a view widely held. It is probably false.

THE ROLE OF THE INDIVIDUAL INVENTOR

Most inventions are obviously made by individuals, in the sense that a creative idea is only likely to emerge from the mind of one person; groups of people do not tend to produce creative ideas, any more than a group of people composes a great symphony. Yet it is obviously no accident that small societies have often produced great men at the same time—the music composed in eighteenth and nineteenth century Vienna, for instance, or the English romantic poets—and so there are apparently sociological bases for invention. What, then, is meant by the phrase 'the individual inventor'? The *pure* case of the individual inventor is a man who works by himself, financing his own activity and deciding the line which his work will follow. If he is successful, the results of his work will, at least in the first instance, belong to him to use as he pleases. Much inventive activity is, of course, a part-time or leisure pursuit of technologists employed by firms. As long as the conditions just stated hold, such people will be called 'individual inventors'. The other extreme will be the corporate or institutional inventor who is a paid employee, hired to work in some particular field, and the results of his work will accrue to the institution or firm that employs him. Between these two extremes there are an infinite number of variations. Consider the university scientist who may be supported in his inventive activity by a firm which, while having prior claim on his inventions, may leave him completely free to decide which avenues to explore. On the other hand, a firm may support his work on the condition that they decide the area of his interest.

This was true in the case of Wankel, who invented the rotary engine. Wankel is usually cited as an example of an individual inventor, yet his work was financed by BMW from 1934–36, by the German Air Ministry from 1936–45 and by NSU after the War. The influence of the car firms on Wankel seems not to have extended beyond determining his main area of work. He worked at his own research institute, and it is on these grounds that he is described as an individual inventor. We can see that between the extremes of the pure individual inventor and the pure corporate inventor, there will be some inventors who have some of the characteristics of each of the extremes. Whether or not these are to be described as individual inventors is a matter of judgement.

First, we consider the relative magnitude of the inventive activity that is undertaken by individuals. In the absence of any data on the relative expenditures made by individual inventors and firms we have to rely on information about outcomes. There are two sources of such information: patent statistics, and qualitative information on important inventions.

Taken at face value, patent statistics indicate a secular decline in the importance of the individual inventor. For the U.K., Jewkes, Sawers and Stillerman found from sample enquiries that firms have been accounting for an increasing proportion of patent applications: 15%, 1913; 58%, 1938; and 68%, 1955.[1] In the U.S.A., the trend is rather erratic, but, since 1900, firms have claimed an increasing proportion of patent applications. However, about 40% of patent applications in the U.S.A. are still made by individuals. The general weaknesses of using patent statistics as a measure of inventive activity have been discussed earlier, but in this context the role of the individual inventor may be understated as inventions may be assigned by individuals to firms before patent applications are made, or granted. Further, as Patent Offices in many countries are becoming overworked, the delay in handling applications may increase the chance of the individual's assigning the rights of an invention to a firm for fear that it would be pirated before being patented, or for more straightforward financial reasons. This would result in a bias in the time series. However, there seems little doubt that the quantitative role of the individual has declined, but that it remains significant still.

[1] J. Jewkes, D. Sawers and R. Stillerman, *op. cit.*, p. 89. It must be remembered that, since 1913, the tax laws have tended to make it increasingly profitable for individuals to turn themselves into companies.

This significance becomes clearer on examining the qualitative evidence. We must first consider how we are to pick out inventions from the host of small changes in products and processes that are being made continually. If we could measure the magnitude of an invention, the task would be easy: we should consider a significant invention to be one of greater than a given magnitude in 'importance', and very small 'inventions' would be classed merely as 'improvements'. An invention has a technical and an economic magnitude; and it has a past and a future, which give four possible dimensions to the magnitude of an invention.[1] First, an invention has a technical past. This will relate to the magnitude of the technical problem overcome by the invention. Clearly, the economist is not the best judge of this magnitude, but it is suggested that on this criterion some inventions (e.g. the hovercraft) are of a greater magnitude than others (e.g. a child-proof car-lock). Secondly, an invention has a technical future. Using this measure, the size of an invention rests upon the number (and size) of subsequent inventions that follow an inventive breakthrough. Thus, the invention of the transistor had a greater technical potential than did the safety match. A third dimension is the economic past of an invention. This comprises the cost of an invention and is measured by the cost of the resources which were used in its creation. Although there are difficulties in assigning costs to any given invention, and while it is not clear how far back in the line of causation we should go, this concept of the magnitude of an invention would seem to have the greatest possibility of practical quantification. Finally, there is the economic future of an invention. A useful invention either permits the production of new goods or enables reductions in cost to occur. Thus, formally, the magnitude of an invention is given by the discounted present value of the additional yield that it will permit. Without entering into a discussion of the problem involved, it is clear that although, as economists, this is the figure we are mostly likely to be interested in we are unlikely to be able to arrive at such figures and that we have to rely on measures of economic cost. (This problem is discussed further in Chapter 8.) Unfortunately, there may be no correlation between the two measures.

In the event, although these possible measures may act as a conceptual framework, we just have to rely on rules of thumb to distinguish the significant from the insignificant inventions. Jewkes, Sawers and Stillerman in their work on invention drew up a list of seventy of (in their judgement) the most important inventions in the twentieth century. Of these, just over half were the results of the work of individual inventors. Some examples are: air-cushion

[1] S. Kuznets *op. cit.*

vehicles (Cockerell); the jet-engine (Whittle); penicillin (Fleming); xerography (Carlson); the rotary engine (Wankel); power-steering (Davis); and cellophane (Brandenberger). From this, it is possible to argue that relatively few major advances come from industrial and commercial laboratories, for about half of the major inventions come from individuals, and there is evidence that universities and government research institutions produce significant numbers of major inventions. The reasons for this pattern, and for the distribution of individual and corporate inventions between industries, will become clear if we examine the forces working in favour of the individual inventor as the major source of inventions.

The first is time. Firms tend to be interested in projects that yield pay-offs within a relatively short period of time. In a much-quoted McGraw-Hill survey of research and development expenditures in the U.S.A., 90% of firms expected their research expenditures to pay-off within five years. As these five years have to cover the whole process of recouping expenditure on research, invention, innovation, and marketing new products, it is clear that on this basis little emphasis can be placed on major advances in basic knowledge. In the pharmaceutical industry, it takes over five years to test a new product and between eight and nine years before it is fully marketed. As a director of research for a pharmaceutical company has said, no research would be undertaken by his company if strict financial criteria were imposed. It is becoming increasingly accepted that the use of modern accounting techniques, such as discounted cash flow, which emphasize the importance of quick results, are inappropriate in this context. Some criteria have to be used, though, and in Chapter 5 we will examine some criteria that have been suggested.

The corollary to this is that much industrial research and development is devoted to small improvements in design and production. A similar tendency might be expected to follow from the uncertainty inherent in the inventive process. By definition, a major invention is something new and hence cannot be carefully planned. It may be expected, but invention is inherently a very uncertain activity. The uncertainty increases with the magnitude of the advance sought. Most firms seek to reduce, or avoid, uncertainty and hence it seems to make sense for them to concentrate on research and development that is aimed at less ambitious and more predictable results. Because of these two reasons, there are *a priori* grounds for expecting a significant proportion of major advances to emanate from sources outside firms. To individual inventors, and to inventors in sponsored research institutes, neither time nor uncertainty pose such severe problems.

Inventors do not charge themselves for their own time and

universities are in like case. Something may hinge on the nature of the remuneration to individual invention, although it does not seem likely that economic forces are of overriding importance. If inventors were risk-averters and wished to earn a steady income from their full- or part-time inventing, then, like firms, they would be attracted to routine improvements rather than fundamental advance. Yet there seems little doubt from psychological studies of the inventor 'type', that they act in precisely the opposite way. A very low probability of a large prize (either in terms of money or academic eminence) is more attractive than the high probability of a small prize. If this is true, then it is to be expected that inventors will not be deterred by the prospect of expending large amounts of time on very uncertain work. In research institutions, similarly, there will be less emphasis on immediate results; but research institutes have to be financed, and in a battle for funds evidence of even modest achievement may be needed. Research and invention are, like writing and painting, creative activities. Profit and loss play their part; but for some people they are compulsive human activities.[1]

A further factor working against invention in a business context is the difficulty of providing the right 'atmosphere'. While firms may be willing to provide funds for research and, at the same time, give research workers a free hand—Carothers's research in polymerization at Du Pont seems to have been relatively unfettered—it is in the nature of commercial firms that they wish to *organize* activities. Organization, and the consequent interference with activities, may be destructive to inventors. Notable advances have often been made by people with uncommitted minds who are willing to explore in random and unexpected directions. Jewkes, Sawers and Stillerman have put it as follows: 'The essential feature of innovation is that the path to it is not known before. The less, therefore, an inventor is pre-committed in his speculations by training and tradition, the better the chance of his escaping from the grooves of accepted thought.'[2] These, then, are the advantages held by the individual inventor.

We have seen, however, that (at least quantitatively) there is no doubt that the individual inventor has declined in relative importance during the twentieth century. The major factor working against him is lack of finance. Much research requires specialized equipment whose cost is beyond the reach of the great majority of individuals, and almost of necessity has to be carried out in industrial laboratories

---

[1] For an analysis which places more emphasis on monetary incentives, see F. Machlup, 'The Supply of Inventors and Inventions', in: *The Rate and Direction of Inventive Activity*, Princeton, Princeton University Press, 1962, pp. 143–67.

[2] J. Jewkes, D. Sawers and R. Stillerman, *op. cit.*, p. 96.

with commercial finance. The importance of finance in many cases may be greater in development than in research. Thus, the individual inventor may assign his invention to a firm for it to undertake the costly process of development. We would therefore expect to find the role of the individual inventor to be of most significance in industries, or activities, which do not use or require large amounts of expensive equipment. There is some evidence that this is so: in the U.K. patent statistics do not distinguish between individual and corporate inventions, but in the U.S.A. individual inventors account for 88% of mechanical inventions, 9% of electrical inventions and 3% of chemical inventions.[1] The high proportion of mechanical inventions accounted for by individual inventors supports the view that individuals largely undertake follow-on inventions which, again, do not require specialized equipment. In principle, of course, if financial markets were perfect, an individual would have as easy access to finance as would a firm; in practice, since most investment is corporately financed, it is upon firms' finance that invention relies.

It has also been suggested that invention *is* a co-operative product, a team activity. Thus, contrary to our argument above that major breakthroughs come from the uncommitted mind prepared to explore in unusual directions, it can be argued that inventions are a result of many highly trained minds working methodically over problems, backed up by large amounts of finance. Clearly, there is truth in both contentions, for major inventions have been the product of both team and individual work.

Schumpeter, Sir John Hicks and David Landes have all laid emphasis on the great, innovative waves that have occurred. There are times when inventions appear to be bunched, as in textiles in the late eighteenth century, steel and chemicals in the late nineteenth century, and in pharmaceuticals in the mid-twentieth century. The origin of such waves is partly illusory, of course, because it is hindsight that makes us say that things which were coincidental are in fact linked, but, even making allowance for it, the weight of evidence strongly supports the wave theory. Probably, as well as a conducive industrial and political atmosphere, some crucial breakthrough is involved which, once made, brings in its wake many further developments.

To summarize, the conclusion we reach is that the individual inventor has declined in relative importance. The major cause of the decline is probably relative lack of finance. Large amounts of capital are now required in many research activities, and the large salaries that firms can offer bring many would-be individual inventors into

[1] R. Nelson, M. Peck and E. Kalachek, *Technology, Economic Growth, and Public Policy*, Washington, Brookings, 1967, p. 58.

industrial laboratories. As a result, the major part of individual, inventive activity may be in making small improvements of a mechanical nature to existing techniques. We have seen, however, that it is a mistake to portray all individual inventors as 'garage' inventors. Men working on their own have been responsible for major breakthroughs, and the very nature of the inventive process suggests that the individual inventor will continue to play a significant role in furthering technological change.

PATENTS

As in all industrial countries, the inventor in the U.K. has the opportunity of preventing others from using or copying his invention without his express permission. Not all inventions are patentable. The Patents Act, 1949, defined invention as 'any manner of new manufacture . . . and any new method of process of testing applicable to the improvement or control of manufacture . . . '. Specifically excluded, then, are theoretical ideas and scientific principles. It is open to any individual or firm to apply for a patent on an invention which comes within the scope of the system. Once a patent is applied for, and a specification deposited at the Patent Office, there is a fairly lengthy procedure by which the Office deals with the application. This procedure falls into two parts. First, there is a 'search' to see if what is claimed to be patentable has been included in previous applications. Secondly, there is an 'examination' which includes ensuring that the application is covered by the Act, and that the description is clear and the patent will not endow too wide a monopoly in relation to the specification. The whole screening process takes between two and three years. Details of the patent are published shortly after it is granted. When a patent is granted, it is valid (as long as renewal-fees are paid) for sixteen years. The recent trend of patents applied for and granted is shown in Table 3.1.

TABLE 3.1. *Patents Applied for and Granted: U.K., 1963–70*

	Applications	Grants
1963	51,468	30,148
1964	53,104	32,169
1965	55,507	33,864
1966	58,471	37,272
1967	59,290	38,999
1968	61,995	43,038
1969	63,614	37,127
1970	62,101	40,004

Source: *Patents, Designs and Trade Markets, 1970*, London, HMSO, 1971.

On the basis of a two-year lag between applications and grants it can be seen that about 70% of patent applications are successful. About 30% of the applications are from U.K. residents. Most patents are not renewed for the full sixteen years, and this can be seen by comparing the level of annual grants of patents (see Table 3.1) with the total number of patents still in force, which is about 240,000.

The patent system as it operates in this country—and in other industrial countries—is an attempt to solve a dilemma which arises from inventive activity. The difficulty is that, once an invention has occurred, society will benefit if details of the invention are freely available to all to copy or use as they wish. If this is the case, however, there is no incentive for individuals or firms to allocate resources to inventive activity, because they will not be able to appropriate the returns. Thus, static resource allocation analysis suggests one policy, while concern for growth and technological advance points to another.[1] Let us examine the dilemma more closely.

It is normally argued that information is a free good in the sense that it is non-rival—i.e. my use of some information does not mean there is less left for you—and in the sense that it is non-appropriable (in the absence of patent laws). If a piece of information is potentially useful to someone in society, and if the costs of transmitting that information are zero, then to obtain an optimal (static) allocation of resources the information should be made available at zero price. Where there are costs in transmitting information, a price should be charged to cover the costs, which will normally be low. This is the argument for making information freely available.

It is not necessarily true that information is a non-rival entity, because the *usefulness* of information may decline with the number of people using it, and it is, of course, possible to keep information secret. In the context of information about inventions it is probably easier to keep secret process inventions than product inventions, although new processes often lie behind new products.[2] If a price (to cover costs of transmission) is charged for information, there is a further problem. A prospective purchaser does not know the value of a piece of information until he has acquired it. Therefore, he has to act on some estimate, perhaps based on past experience, of its likely value to him. It has been suggested that this will tend, at any

---

[1] This is, of course, a not unfamiliar problem in economics. The utility-theorists, for example, were led to advocate equality of income, because that would maximize utility, and to advocate inequality of income in order to generate the saving necessary for capital accumulation and growth.

[2] Thus, some firms spend considerable sums on examining a rival's products in an effort to see how they are produced.

given price, to lead to a less than optimal demand at that price.[1] There exists, then, a case based on static resource allocation analysis, for the free dissemination of information concerning inventions.

The case for conferring a monopoly upon the owner of an invention stems from the reasonable view that the greater the returns from inventive activity, the greater the amount that will be undertaken. The more inventive activity there is, the greater will be the number and magnitude of inventions. Given that inventions are a 'good thing', society will benefit from granting absolute rights to those who produce inventions. If information about inventions were made freely available, the inventor, it is argued, would not be able to appropriate the rewards of the invention. The incentive to undertake such activity will be much reduced. It follows, from our discussion of individual inventors, that this argument will be strongest in the case of corporate inventors.

Society, in order to induce inventive activity, has therefore to give the inventor monopoly rights. It has been suggested that this traditional argument is too simple, and that there are other rewards that the inventor can capture. Hirshleifer draws the distinction between *foreknowledge*—the ability to predict successfully, and *discovery*—defined as: 'correct recognition of something that possibly already exists, though hidden from view'.[2] Although individuals, and society, can gain from both sorts of knowledge, it is with discovery that we are concerned here. The argument runs as follows. An invention shifts the technological possibilities facing society. A process-invention shifts marginal costs downwards, and with free information these gains will accrue to society. Such technological changes are reflected in changes in market prices and the market valuation of certain assets may change. An example is Whitney's cotton gin. The technological effects of this development were an expansion in the production and consumption of cotton. There were also, however, pecuniary effects: 'The cotton gin had obvious speculative implications for the price of cotton, the value of slaves and of cotton bearing land, the business prospects of firms engaged in cotton warehousing and shipping, and the site values of key points in the transport network that sprang up.' In fact, Whitney had one of the first patents, but it was not effective and many others used his idea. He did not apparently make any speculative gains though he was ideally placed to do so.

[1] K. Arrow, 'Economic Welfare and the Allocation of Resources for Invention', in: *The Rate and Direction of Inventive Activity*, Princeton, Princeton University Press, 1962.
[2] J. Hirshleifer, 'The Private and Social Value of Information and the Reward to Inventive Activity', *American Economic Review*, 1971.

It is suggested on this basis that the technological benefits will be maximized if the relevant information is freely available. These benefits, however, will be reflected in asset valuations and the inventor can profitably speculate on these.[1] There is, however, no presumption that the size of the technological benefits of an invention is related to the magnitude of the speculative opportunities. Therefore, it may follow that some patent protection is necessary for the inventors. But the case for patent protection is weakened and there is, in fact, no strong reason to suppose that there will be, in the absence of patents, an under-investment in inventive activity.

The patent system as it exists strikes some sort of compromise between the case for making information about inventions widely available at low cost, and the case for rewarding the inventor with some monopoly profit. The possibility of speculative gains does not appear to have been recognized. The system appears at first sight to be biased towards the inventor. For example, the first sentence of the report of the Committee which examined the U.K. patent system, in 1970, reads: 'The primary intention of the patent system is the encouragement of new industries in the country.'[2] It is a compromise, however, for two reasons. First, the details of the patent specification are published as soon as the patent is granted, and it is argued that this facilitates associated inventions and perhaps 'follow-on' inventions. In other cases, publication of the patent specification may prevent other people from wastefully duplicating research effort. The point is, then, that the information is made available, and although the owner retains property rights in it so that others cannot directly make use of it, they nevertheless may reap benefits from it (or avoid costs that they would otherwise incur).

Secondly, and less important, only a temporary monopoly is conferred. The Report on the patent system quotes in this context from T. A. Blanco White: 'The temporary monopoly is not objectionable, for if it had not been for the inventor who devised and disclosed the improvement nobody would have been able to use it at that or any other time, since nobody would have known about it. Furthermore, the giving of the monopoly encourages the putting into practice of the invention, for the only way the inventor can make a profit from it is by putting it into practice: either ... himself ... or by

[1] The 'technological', 'pecuniary' terminology is due to McKean, who suggested the distinction for use in cost-benefit analysis. Technological spillovers from a project should be included in an appraisal, but pecuniary spillovers should not. They are simply a reflection of the benefits in market valuations and to include them would be to double-count. Thus, a petrol-station sited at the access to a newly constructed road-bridge will increase its profits and its site value will increase. This merely reflects the benefit of additional journeys.

[2] *The British Patent System*, London, HMSO, 1971, p. 1.

allowing others to use it in return for royalties.'[1] The first of these contentions is based on a view of the advance of scientific and technological knowledge that is not supported by the facts (see Chapter 8). Nor is the second contention very firmly based. One argument put forward against the patent system is that the holders of patents do not use them because they may reduce, or eliminate, the economic rents earned on previous investment, and it may be more profitable to retain existing methods.

This latter comment serves to emphasize that in considering the relative advantages and disadvantages of the patent system, we must look at the extent to which the monopoly positions endowed by patents are abused. That is, the social costs of the patent system are not confined to the misallocation of resources due to restrictions on the flow of information. The monopoly position that is protected by a patent is in some senses stronger than that given by other things. Monopolies exist because there are various factors that operate to restrict entry into some markets. Most of these restrictions, such as high capital costs of entry, and selling at a loss for extended periods, are relative in the sense that at some level of monopoly profit other firms would enter. The restriction imposed by a patent, however, can be an absolute one, a restriction enforceable by law. The most obvious way in which such a position is exploited is through higher prices than would prevail if some form of competition existed.[2] Firms may purchase patents on related processes in order to prevent potential competitors producing by alternative means, and they may protect weak patents through clauses in licensing arrangements on strong patents. Although under the patent laws firms cannot force the purchase of certain goods or forbid the use of certain processes through licensing arrangements, there is a large number of restrictions that may be imposed. For example, the terms of a licence may include the avoidance of certain markets. Moreover, such agreements between firms are exempt from the Restrictive Trade Practices Act, 1956, and 1968. The use of restrictive terms in licence agreements is thought to be particularly prevalent in the U.K.[3] The dangers of one firm attempting to gain a hold on some processes through patents are greatest when a whole industrial sector becomes dominated in this way. If the result is purely protective action by the monopolist, then, of course, the whole point of the patent system—that it leads to technological advance—is lost. Against some of these arguments, however, must be set the factor that patents have in the past enabled

[1] HMSO, *op. cit.*
[2] Higher, that is, by an amount greater than that necessary to cover costs of (and normal profits on) inventive activity.
[3] A. Silberston, 'The Patent System', *Lloyds Bank Review*, 1967.

firms to break into areas previously dominated by one or two firms. It has to be admitted that little is known about the extent of such practices in the U.K., but the dangers are clearly there.

Theoretically, the patent system would be deemed beneficial, if the social benefits from the extra inventive activity induced by the patent laws exceeded or were equal to the social costs of the system. This way of putting things is not a great help in practice, because there is no clear way of estimating the costs and benefits. The general consensus seems to be, however, that the patent system should continue in more or less its present form.

One alternative that has been proposed is that the inventor (individual or corporate) should be paid a lump sum equal to the profits he would have obtained, had he had sole use of his invention. The invention would then be freely available for all to use. But it is usually accepted that this proposal would be enormously difficult to operate in practice. To the extent that inventors take advantage of speculative positions, Hirshleifer's analysis would suggest that this transfer of wealth would take place without the need for government intervention. In this case, of course, the proposal does not have to be 'operated'.

The Committee set up to examine the patent system and patent law found that all the evidence it received was in favour (in principle) of the system and proposals centred upon improving it: 'No alternative scheme was put to us.'[1] The Committee's recommendations largely concerned the operation and administration of the patent system, although it did, in addition, advocate an extension of the validity of patents to twenty years. The not unreasonable view was taken that problems associated with restrictive terms in licenses, and exploitation of patent monopolies, should be dealt with through restrictive practices legislation rather than the patent laws. It is important to note, however, that the Committee did have very much in mind, throughout their deliberations, the international aspects of the system: 'If patents were solely a national affair it might be that some other system might emerge.'[2] It gave no indication, however, as to what that system would be.

[1] HMSO, *op. cit.*, p. 13.　　　　　　　　[2] HMSO, *op. cit.*

CHAPTER 4

Research and Development Expenditure in Manufacturing Industry

In this chapter and Chapter 5, we move away from the individual to the firm. There are many important and interesting questions to be considered in any analysis of industrial research and development. Some of the questions which we discuss are whether large firms spend, proportionately to their size, more on research and development than small firms, and which market structure leads to the highest research and development expenditure. What are the motives behind research expenditure? How do firms decide how much to spend on research?

Overlying all these influences on research and development expenditure is, however, the effect of the industry in which the firm is located. Because the nature of an industry influences, apart from its research expenditure, the market structure, and the average size of firm, there is an obvious danger in an industry of the causal relationships becoming confused. Therefore, the first task is to describe the industrial pattern of research and development expenditure. In Chapter 5 we take up the other issues raised above, which relate to individual firms and markets.

EXPENDITURE ON RESEARCH AND DEVELOPMENT

In 1967, £507 million was spent on research and development *within* —but not *by*—private industry. Of this total, nearly £502 million was in manufacturing industry, nearly £4 million in construction, and £2 million in all other industries. We therefore propose to concentrate on manufacturing industry. Other industries benefit from this expenditure and, as will become clear when we discuss innovation, exert considerable influence on the effectiveness of this expenditure.

Table 4.1 gives the distribution of research expenditure within manufacturing industry. It is essential in interpreting this information to realize that the notion of an 'industry' is a generalization and that the precise functions which are included in research and development may differ between industries. It must also be emphasized that these

TABLE 4.1. *Current Expenditure on Research and Development: U.K. Manufacturing Industry, 1967**

	(1) Expenditure Within Manufacturing Industry (£m.)	(2) Percentage of Total	(3) Expenditure Financed by Private Industry (£m.)	(4) Percentage of Total
Food, drink and tobacco	14·7	2·9	19·5	5·4
Chemicals	70·1	14·0	78·0	21·3
Metal manufacture	7·9	1·6	8·5	2·3
Mechanical engineering†	54·0	10·7	47·5	13·0
Scientific instruments	11·9	2·4	10·4	2·9
Electronics	100·6	20·0	49·7	13·6
Other electrical engineering	28·0	5·6	28·9	7·9
Aerospace	146·6	29·2	36·1	9·9
Vehicles and shipbuilding	35·1	7·0	46·7	12·8
Textiles, leather and clothing	10·5	2·1	12·2	3·3
Other manufacturing	22·4	4·5	26·8	7·4
Total	501·8	100·0	364·3	99·8

Source: See Table 2.1, pp. 18, 28.
* The apparent paradox that some figures in column (3) are greater than those in column (1) is largely due to under-reporting. For details see source, p. 7.
† Mechanical engineering includes 'metal products not elsewhere specified'.

D

expenditures cannot be equated with inventive activity and can only serve as one rough indicator of the scale of such activities.

The first two columns (Table 4.1) relate to expenditure within each industry. There is a heavy concentration of expenditure in certain industries. Two industries, aerospace and electronics, account for nearly half of the total and these two industries together with chemicals and mechanical engineering account for about three-quarters of the total.

Nearly £200 million of expenditure within manufacturing industry is financed by the government. Moreover, government finance is heavily biased towards certain industries, 90% going to electronics and aerospace. Therefore, there is a more even distribution of research and development which is both located in and financed by private manufacturing industry. Thus, from column (4) of the table, it can be seen that aerospace and electronics account for only 23·5% of research expenditure financed by private industry, compared with 49·2% of research expenditure located within industry. As far as possible, we wish to discuss the expenditure of the public sector in another chapter.

On either basis, certain industries spend more on research and development than do others; that much is clear. We can get a closer picture of what is termed the 'research intensiveness' of different industries by relating research and development expenditures to net output. The net output of an industry is the sum of wages, salaries, and gross trading profits. In Table 4.2, we show research intensiveness calculated on two bases—using figures for total expenditure and for expenditure financed by industry.

The greatest inter-industry differences appear, of course, when all expenditure, whatever the source of finance, is considered. At one extreme, the aerospace industry's research and development effort is nearly 30% of its net output, whereas in food, metal manufacture, textiles, and 'other manufacturing' the proportion is less than 1%. These disparities are much softened when industry financed expenditures only are considered; but the fact remains that some industries are much more research intensive than others.

It is known that a similar distribution of research expenditures, and a similar pattern of research intensiveness, obtains in most industrialized countries. Presumably because of the pattern of government support, the distribution of research and development expenditures in the U.S.A. appears to be more or less the same as that in the U.K. Although there are some differences, the research intensive industries tend to be the same in each country. These industries are aerospace, electrical and mechanical engineering, chemicals, and scientific instruments. In most industrial countries this group of

TABLE 4.2. *Research intensiveness of Manufacturing Industry: U.K.**

	Research and Development Expenditure as a Percentage of Net Output Using:	
	(1) Research Expenditure Within Each Industry	(2) Research Expenditure Located in and Financed by Each Industry
Food, drink and tobacco	0·7	1·0
Chemicals	4.5	5·0
Metal manufacture	0·7	0·8
Mechanical engineering	1·8	1·6
Scientific instruments	4·3	3·8
Electronics	16·3	8·1
Other electrical engineering	3·5	3·7
Aerospace	29·9	7·4
Vehicles and shipbuilding	2·4	3·2
Textiles, leather and clothing	0·6	0·7
Other manufacturing	0·8	0·9

Sources: See Table 2.1.
Census of Production, 1968.

* Net output figures are for 1968, research expenditures are for 1967/8.

industries accounts for a large proportion of industrial research and development expenditures.

Table 4.3 shows that manufacturing is responsible for the greater part of research expenditure and that the research intensive industries as a group dominate the research effort in manufacturing. The relative importance of each research intensive industry varies from country to country. This is partly due to the differing incidence of government finance, especially in the case of the aircraft industry.

The dominance of a few sectors of manufacturing industry is also apparent when the two other indicators of research activity are used. The distribution of qualified scientists and engineers employed on research and development work in manufacturing industry is shown in Table 4.4.

The industrial classification does not correspond exactly to that used in Table 4.1, but four industries—chemicals, mechanical engineering, electronics, and aircraft—account for 70% of the total employment of qualified scientists and engineers.

Patent statistics are less satisfactory for comparative purposes, because there may be marked inter-industry differences in the propensity to a patent of a new product or process. However, the same

TABLE 4.3. *Shares of All Intra-mural Industrial Research and Development, 1963*

	Belgium	Canada	France	Germany	Italy	Japan	Sweden	U.K.	U.S.A.
Chemicals	41·9	21·9	17·9	32·0	25·7	26·2	9·4	13·2	12·1
Mechanical engineering	4·7	3·9 ⎫	4·9 ⎫	n.a.	7·1	4·9	13·2	6·4	7·7
Instruments	1·5	2·7 ⎬	⎬		2·7 ⎫	26·0	0·5	2·1	3·6
Electrical engineering	15·0	21·9	26·0	28·2	22·6 ⎬		22·5	19·8	19·7
Aircraft	1·4	15·7	22·4	—	n.a.	—	18·6	28·4	38·2
All manufacturing	92·9	90·4	89·3	91·7	88·2	92·9	94·6	91·3	97·5

Source: See Table 2.2, source, pp. 98–9.

TABLE 4.4 *Distribution of Qualified Scientists and Engineers in Manufacturing: U.K., 1968*

	Number	Percentage of Total
Food, drink and tobacco	1,373	3·6
Chemicals	9,545	24·9
Metal manufacture	1,755	4·6
Mechanical engineering	5,063	13·2
Electronics	8,080	21·0
Other electrical engineering	2,460	6·4
Aircraft	4,323	11·3
Vehicles	1,049	2·7
Textiles, leather and clothing	1,726	4·5
Other manufacturing	2,940	7·7
Total	38,314	99·9

Source: See Table 2.1, source, p. 118.

dominance of a few industries emerges. In 1968, chemicals, mechanical and electrical engineering, and vehicles accounted for 81% of patent specifications published by manufacturing industry.

There are two apparently conflicting explanations for the distribution of research and development efforts—'technology push' and 'demand pull.' The technology push argument is based on the view that technology offers the greatest scope for advance and profit in a small group of industries—the science based industries. In industries with a complex and advanced technological base, the chances of making further *technical* advance is high, provided that the underlying scientific ideas are widely and generally known. These industries are usually capital goods and consumer durable goods industries, whose customers are more likely to place value upon technical excellence and 'newness' than are consumers of other products. These two factors combine to yield a relatively high *economic* return to research and development expenditure. The market structure of such industries may also be favourable to research and development. In so far as there is any truth in the contention that large firms spend proportionately more on research and development than small firms, then, as there are significant economies of scale in science based, capital goods industries, the nature of the industrial structure affects research and development expenditure in this way as well.[1]

The contrary 'demand pull' view is largely based on the work of Jacob Schmookler.[2] His results are based on an analysis of patent

[1] This contention is discussed below. There is support for it, but the evidence does not support the simple view that large firms spend proportionately more on research and development over all size ranges.

[2] J. Schmookler, *Invention and Economic Growth*, London, Harvard University Press, 1966.

statistics. It must be remembered that although we have used patents and research and development expenditures as two indicators of the scale of activities aimed at securing scientific and technological advance, these two series should not be confused. Figures of research and development expenditure reflect inputs into a process, while figures of patents measure only *one* of the outputs of the process. For most research and development expenditure is not made with the object of securing a patentable invention. Schmookler's results show that, for the U.S.A., the state of demand in capital goods industries determined inventive activity. Inventive activity in these industries follows, rather than leads, investment as far as can be seen from the time series. Schmookler explains these findings as follows: invention is pursued for economic gain; the gain varies with the expected sales, and these expectations are based on current sales of capital goods. This is a very simplified version of the argument. The role of time lags, for example, in this process has to be taken into account.

Support for Schmookler's argument is to be found in empirical studies of industrial *innovation*. This is not the same thing, of course, but the stimuli to innovation must exert some influence on invention. Four empirical studies found that between two-thirds and three-quarters of industrial innovations were stimulated by a recognition of production and market need rather than by technological opportunity.[1]

These findings, and those of Schmookler, are not necessarily inconsistent with the technology push explanation. An emphasis on demand factors need not deny the importance of technological factors operating on the supply side.[2]

A demand pressure emanating from consumer goods industries may be reflected in inventive activity in capital goods industries, because there are special technological factors which make research and development most profitable there. This is, indeed, probably the case. Next, Schmookler refutes the view that technological advance is an exogenous variable. In his work, it is endogenous to economic models, because it is influenced by demand. But this is surely not to deny the importance of science in determining the path of technological advance, nor is it to deny that it is most profitable to concentrate technological change in capital goods industries for technological reasons. Thirdly, Schmookler's results are based on patent

---

[1] *The Conditions for Success in Technological Innovation*, Paris, OECD, 1971, p. 32.
[2] R. Matthews, 'The Contribution of Science and Technology to Economic Development', in: *The Role of Science and Technology in Economic Development*, Paris, UNESCO, 1970.

statistics, and the use of such statistics to reflect inventive activity has been severely criticized.[1] There is therefore a qualitative problem. Two of the four studies mentioned earlier found that most radical innovations were located in the research intensive industries and that their frequency was greater there. At least some of the apparent inconsistency between the two assertions may be due to one suggestion being based on figures of research and development expenditure and the other being based on an analysis of patent statistics.

There is finally the argument that the high level of research and development expenditures in certain industries may simply reflect the high cost of achieving results which are necessary for competitive reasons. That is to say, in an oligopolistic situation a firm may have to undertake research and development to keep up with, or overtake, its rivals (who are acting similarly), even though its rate of return on such activity is lower than it would be in competitive or monopolistic conditions. It seems that, although market stimuli are important in determining the direction of inventive and innovative activity *within* an industry or firm, technological factors are more important in determining the distribution of research expenditure *between* industries.

It is not only technological factors which determine the industrial distribution of research expenditures. Little effort will be put into research and development, even where technical advances are thought likely, if these advances would result in small cost savings or if it was not possible to significantly enlarge existing markets with a new product. The similarity of research and development concentration in the same few industries in most industrial countries seems, however, to support the view that technological factors are important in determining the industrial distribution of these expenditures, since the technological conditions are similar but the demand and market conditions are not.

Research and development expenditure is concentrated, then, in a few industries. Nevertheless, the results of this expenditure spread to a large number of other industries, both within and outside manufacturing. The mechanism operates by inter-firm purchases of materials and equipment, particularly capital equipment. The research intensive industries are basically producer goods industries, and hence the benefits of their research are spread over many other sectors. Large productivity gains have been made possible in agriculture by new chemical products and to a lesser extent by research and development in the mechanical engineering industry.

[1] See, e.g. B. Sanders, 'Some Difficulties in Measuring Inventive Activity', in: *The Rate and Direction of Inventive Activity*, Princeton, Princeton University Press, 1962.

The textile industry has been revitalized by the advent of man-made fibres developed in the chemical industry, and the computer and specialized office machinery have transformed many operations in the service industries. We shall discuss this diffusion process more fully later—as it more properly belongs to an analysis of innovation —but there are two more points which should be made here.

Because the benefits of research expenditures are felt in industries other than those in which they are undertaken, a low ratio of research and development to net output in an industry does not mean that more *ought* to be spent on research and development by the industry in question. It may be better from the point of view of resource allocation to concentrate such expenditure in the science based industries—with other industries purchasing the results in the form of producer goods and materials.

This is not to argue a case for no research expenditure on the part of some industries. The employment of qualified scientists and engineers, for example, may be a necessary condition for choosing the most appropriate capital goods and other intermediate goods. Development work will be necessary on processes which are potentially, but not at present exactly suited to the purchasing industry. Internal research and development is thus a useful and often essential complement to that done by supplying industries. Where purchasing firms are very backward in appreciating the potential of technological advance in supplying firms, the incentive to advance in the supplier may be weakened. In this context, the number of qualified scientists and engineers employed in production as well as in research and development assumes considerable significance. It follows, too, that a producer goods industry may have to carry out research in other industries in order to discover new uses for its products. An example is the current research of IBM into such diverse problems as atmospheric pollution, the conduction of electricity through semiconductors, the evolution of galaxies, the sources of weather, and the ageing of genes.

ALLOCATION OF RESEARCH AND DEVELOPMENT EXPENDITURES

The set of activities categorized as 'research and development' have so far been treated as a composite group. We now briefly consider the relative importance of basic research, applied research and development. In 1967, in manufacturing industry the proportionate allocation of expenditure was as follows: basic research, 3%; applied research, 19%; and development, 78%. There was considerable variation between industries, although in every industry (save one) the ranking was as given in these figures. The exception was pharmaceutical products, where applied research accounted for two-thirds of expenditure. In the other research intensive industries, development claimed an above-average share of resources.

Only 3% of industry's research and development expenditures, then, are in basic research. Most basic research occurs, in fact, outside industry. In 1967, 20% of basic research took place in the industrial sector, compared with 40% undertaken in the universities, 35% in the government sector and 5% in other organizations.

The main reason for the apparent reluctance of firms to devote many resources to basic research is suggested by the statisticians' definitions. Basic research is 'work undertaken for the advancement of knowledge without specific commercial objectives'. It is not unduly cynical to expect to find firms rarely undertaking activities which have no direct commercial objectives, and, hence, the reason why so little is spent on basic research is clear. But this is only part of the answer, for basic research may yield results which the firm can eventually profitably develop. This must necessarily be so or firms presumably would devote still fewer resources to basic research.

There are numerous strategies, of course, Some basic research is supported by firms because they think they ought to, or they admire the man who does it. 'Student', the statistician, worked for Guinness; his results were useful for batch control, but the firm was proud of him. The Post Office vigorously encourages basic research in telecommunications, even though it has a monopoly, because it feels a public duty to do so. In pharmaceuticals, research is stepped up when profits fall, because large profits can be made from a 'breakthrough' which defeats rival firms, and a breakthrough may be only a one in five thousand chance of many research projects. Firms generally seek to be profit-maximizing, but often they do not know how best to maximize profits and erroneously attach too great a weight to the likely profitable results of a basic research breakthrough.

A great deal depends upon who controls the firm and how it is financed. Research and development is normally an allowable expense against tax. Sometimes it attracts grants. Sometimes, as in the U.S.A., if the research unit is cast in the form of a charitable foundation, it has enabled control of the firm to be exercised by the family while excusing them from all capital, inheritance and income taxes. A firm which has been the creation of one man, or a family, and remains in family ownership, may establish a tradition of high research activity (like Pilkingtons).

Public esteem undoubtedly plays its part. A major public corporation, like the Post Office, may pride itself upon its high tradition of research, as a great teaching hospital does. A firm controlled to some degree by scientists and technologists—ICI springs to mind, in respect of some of its major Divisions—will feel obliged to devote itself in part to research. In the U.S.A., the Protestant tradition, that thanks are given to the Creator by understanding His works, has been strong until recently, and a firm or family will found or endow a university (like Stanford or the Rockefeller Institute); and in the U.K. also, Nuffield and Wolfson Colleges express the public concerns of their founders. Firms are surprisingly high-minded on occasions.

So, there are a variety of reasons why some basic research is under-taken by industry. The fact remains, however, that the bulk of industry's research effort is aimed, not at basic research, but at applied research and development. There are four reasons for this. First, there is the problem of appropriability. The results of basic research (i.e. additions to the stock of scientific knowledge) are not patentable and tend to be disseminated rapidly through communica-tion between scientists. Although, theoretically, the financing firm could prevent or delay such spread of knowledge, it appears that this rarely happens. If firms wish to attract first-class scientists, they have to accept that for reasons of personal prestige, and because there is a long tradition of publication, the scientist will not accept restrictions on the dissemination of research findings. Thus, in practice, research results are something in the nature of a free good. In any case, as has been said, multiple discovery is the scientific norm.

The results of basic research spread faster and are less appropriable than those of applied research. As the firm is interested mainly in the returns to expenditure that it can capture for itself, it follows that there is less incentive to devote resources to basic research than applied research. The low degree of appropriability of the results of basic research sets up the presumption that the private sector, left to itself, would tend to under-invest in basic research, because the social returns may be greater than the private returns. This possibility is discussed in Chapter 8.

Secondly, the uncertainty attached to basic research is high— almost by definition. Adding to knowledge is essentially a process whose results are difficult to forecast, and discoveries arise on an almost random basis, often not being the original object of the research. Thirdly, the pay-offs from basic research may occur many years subsequent to the original expenditure. The methods of investment appraisal used by many firms mean that the long time lags and the uncertainty of research put them low in a firm's range of possible expenditure opportunities. Many research directors probably find their opportunities because their true costs are hidden in conventional accounting systems.

Finally, from a scientific point of view, an industrial research laboratory may not be the best place to undertake a programme of basic research. We have already seen that the atmosphere in industrial laboratories, their organization and administration, may be antipathetic to some creative minds.

Thus, for the above reasons, it may make more sense for many firms to undertake little in the way of basic research, but rather devote their research resources to attempting to apply basic research results emanating elsewhere, to their own particular needs. It is important to note that some employment of scientists in basic research by a firm is necessary, in order that published research findings can be sifted and those most promising for the firm selected as candidates for attention from applied research. Expenditure on basic research is also useful for tackling problems encountered in a firm's applied research. Basic research, then, serves these two important functions, even where the firm is not aiming directly at making significant advances in scientific knowledge. Of course, most basic research is financed by universities and other public bodies. If it were not, industry would presumably play a greater role than it does. But this is idle speculation.

CHAPTER 5

Research and Development in the Firm

In this chapter we are still concerned with research and development in manufacturing industry, but here the emphasis is on the firm rather than, as in previous chapters, on the industry. The chapter is divided into four sections. In the first we examine the relationship between the size of a firm and the scale of its research and development activities. We then look at how research and development expenditures by firms are determined and the problems posed by the relatively high risk and uncertainty encountered in these activities. This question throws some additional light on the issues examined in the first section. Many firms strive to grow, and in the third part of the chapter we look at the part played by research and development in furthering the growth of firms. Finally, we briefly look at the influence of market structure on the scale of firms' research and development expenditures.

RESEARCH AND DEVELOPMENT ACTIVITIES AND THE SIZE OF FIRM

Is there a relationship between the size of firms and their inventive activity? Is it true, for example, that—as Schumpeter and Galbraith have argued—large firms spend more on research and development in relation to their size than do small firms? It is very important to be clear about the question asked. It is known that industrial research and development is concentrated in large firms and that this concentration is greater in research and development than in, for example, employment. In manufacturing in the U.S.A. in 1961, firms with over 5,000 employees accounted for 86% of research and development expenditure but for only 41% of employment and 47% of sales. Information on European countries is fragmentary, but it is known that in 1963, in each of nine OECD countries, the four largest spenders on research and development accounted for at least 20% of all such expenditure in industry. This concentration, however, is largely due to the inter-industry distribution of research and development ex-

60

penditures, described in Chapter 4. In those industries which undertake the largest proportion of research and development—i.e. aerospace, electrical engineering and chemicals—the big firm is typical. It does not follow that such firms spent a great deal on research and development because they are large: it might well be the other way round. It is more likely, then, that the science based nature of these industries both encourages research and development and, through economies of scale, favours the growth of large units of production and marketing. The question is more clearly put as follows: it is true that *within an industry* large firms spend more on research and development in relation to (say) sales, or employment, or assets, than small firms do?

The empirical evidence is at first sight confusing, and unfortunately some of the evidence relates to innovation rather than invention. Such evidence may be useful in this context where the inventing firm and the innovating firm are the same, but the extent to which this is true is not clear. Some caution is therefore necessary. In the U.K., in 1955, there appeared to be no consistent connection between research and development expenditure as a proportion of total assets and size of firm in any of the industry groups surveyed.[1] In the U.S.A., similarly, there seems to be no obvious tendency for large firms to spend more on research and development as a proportion of net sales. The figures are given in Table 5.1, which has to be interpreted carefully.

The data relate only to companies undertaking research and development. No clear picture emerges. The column relating to all manufacturing industries in the table shows that the largest firms, those employing over 10,000 people, had the highest ratio of research and development expenditure to net sales. The totals are heavily influenced by the figures for aerospace, however, and a more reliable picture is gained by looking at each industry separately. Although in one-half of the industries the very largest firms had the highest ratios of research and development expenditure to net sales, there is no obvious pattern in the other size groups. It is interesting to note that in two of the research intensive industries—pharmaceuticals, and scientific instruments—medium sized firms had the highest ratio. In two other research intensive industries—electrical engineering and aerospace—research intensity increases with employment over the four employment ranges.

In France, the ratio of research and development expenditures to sales was higher in small firms *performing research and development* than in large firms. This was true on average and also in most research intensive industries—i.e. electrical engineering, electronics,

[1] J. Jewkes, D. Sawers, and R. Stillerman, *op. cit.*, p. 124.

TABLE 5.1. *Research and Development Expenditures as a Percentage of Net Sales in Companies Undertaking Research and Development: U.S.A., 1968**

	All Firms	Less than 1,000	1,000 to 4,999	5,000 to 9,999	Over 10,000
Food	0·4	0·2	0·4	0·3	0·5
Industrial chemicals	4·1	2·7	3·3	1·5	4·3
Pharmaceuticals	6·2	n.a.	5·7	8·6	5·1
Other chemicals	2·3	n.a.	2·7	1·6	2·7
Oil	1·0	n.a.	0·7	0·6	1·1
Rubber products	2·2	2·2	1·0	2·8	2·2
Stone, clay and glass products	1·9	n.a.	0·9	1·1	2·4
Metal manufacture	0·8	0·8	0·9	0·6	0·8
Metal products	1·3	0·9	1·1	1·4	1·5
Machinery	4·4	2·0	1·9	2·0	6·2
Electrical engineering	8·3	3·8	4·3	4·9	9·7
Motor vehicles	3·2	3·3	1·4	1·7	3·3
Aerospace	19·3	4·3	7·8	9·9	20·2
Scientific instruments	5·9	4·7	2·2	8·1	6·4
Other manufacturing	0·6	n.a.	0·9	0·4	0·7
Total	4·1	2·0	1·7	2·1	4·9

Source: *Research and Development in Industry, 1968*, Washington, 1970, p. 61.
* Three industries for which little information was available have been omitted from the table.

scientific instruments, mechanical engineering, and chemicals (including pharmaceuticals).[1]

Detailed studies of industrial research and development have failed to produce very clear cut results. Scherer examined the relationship between corporate size and inventive activity, using patents and research and development employment as indicators of inventive activity.[2] Both patents and research-employment were found by Scherer to be less concentrated than were sales. This result is apparently at odds with the National Science Foundation statistics, referred to earlier, which show that research and development expenditure is more highly concentrated than sales or employment. Scherer suggests three explanations. First, government contracted research and development does not lead to many patents and is con-

[1] Cited in: *The Conditions for Success in Technological Innovation*, Paris, OECD, 1971, p. 35.
[2] R. Scherer, 'Firm Size, Market Structure, Opportunity and the Output of Patented Inventions', *American Economic Review*, 1965.

centrated in large firms. Secondly, small firms obtain a higher proportion of their patents from non research and development employees; and, finally, small firms apparently conduct their research with the greatest cost consciousness. Relating patents to sales, this study found that in the research intensive industries there were increasing returns up to sales of around $500 million and decreasing returns thereafter. In other industries, the number of patents increased more slowly than did sales over all ranges.

In pharmaceuticals there seems to be a heavy concentration of *innovations* in large firms, and this also seems to be the case in petroleum and coal. From studies in other industries, it seems that big firms have not been a disproportionately large source either of inventions or innovations.

What are the main conclusions that can be drawn from this evidence? The first point is that there is some minimum size of firm below which it is not worth undertaking any research and development—at least that can be identified as such. This, by its nature, is not a conclusion that shows up in the sort of statistics that we have considered. There seems little doubt, however, that it is so. The reasoning is as follows. A scientist, with support facilities, costs something around £10,000 in the U.K. in 1971. It is generally thought unlikely that a firm will devote more than 1·5% of its costs to research and development, so that annual costs of £1½ million represent some such absolute minimum. That is not to say that firms of less than a certain size will spend nothing, for firms are so arbitrary in their definition of what constitutes research and development that some expenditure may appear almost anywhere in the statistics. Some activities of production engineers, for example, may be classed as 'development' when they are not, and some development work may appear as 'overheads'.[1]

Secondly, large firms undertake the major part of all industrial research and development. In the U.S.A., the 300 largest companies account for 92% of research expenditure and the 40 largest companies account for 70%. A similar concentration is thought to hold in the U.K. Therefore, any analysis of industrial research must concentrate on the activities of large firms.

Thirdly, the larger the company, the more likely it is that it will have *some* research activities. In the U.S.A., virtually all firms with over 5,000 employees undertake some research, while only one in ten

---

[1] It has constantly to be borne in mind that research and development covers a multitude of activities. An anecdote may serve to illustrate this. A manager was discussing how activities are allocated to research and development: 'If Jack is asked to repair a machine and he succeeds, it's maintenance. If he fails, it's research.'

of companies with under 500 employees do so. It will be remembered that the statistics in Table 5.1 relate only to firms undertaking research and development.

Fourthly, of the companies who do spend money on research, it does not seem in general to be true that large firms are more research intensive than medium sized firms are.

Fifthly, although the great bulk of research and development takes place in large firms, significant inventions have emanated from small firms and, as we saw in Chapter 3, from individuals. A classic case is xerography. The process was patented, in 1940, by an individual, Carlson, who subsequently approached a number of companies to see if they were interested in developing it. All the major office equipment companies turned him down, but eventually a small photographic company, Haloid, took up the invention. Subsequently, the corporation experienced very rapid growth and, by 1968, Xerox Corporation, as it is now named, ranked 109th in the Fortune list. Many other examples could be cited.[1]

Individuals, small-, medium- and large-sized firms may practise some division of labour in research and development. Since research is more uncertain than development, large firms may be prepared to let inventions occur outside the firm and purchase them for development. This view is consistent with the fact that individuals have been responsible for a significant number of important inventions. This tendency is reinforced by the high (and growing) costs of developing inventions, and the generally high cost of development relative to the costs of research. Such costs effectively put development out of the reach of the individual and, in some cases, of the small firm. The potentially high costs of development may be seen from two examples: ICI spent £4 million developing Terylene (1941–49); and Beecham's spent £9½ million on developing semi-synthetic penicillins (1957–66). In the latter case the research cost £2½ million (1947–57).[2] Further, the average level of development costs is rising, quite apart from reasons associated with increases in the general price level. In many activities, government regulations for safety and environmental purposes have increased the costs of development substantially. In pharmaceuticals, for example, the thalidomide disaster, in which tranquillizers taken by pregnant women led to subsequent births of deformed children, has given rise to safety regulations which have doubled some development costs. More generally, as the stock of technical knowledge increases, the amount of useful effort that can be expected to yield positive returns on development increases. Firms who buy the research efforts of individuals may be making a rational

---

[1] See J. Jewkes, D. Sawers and R. Stillerman, *op. cit.*, p. 207.
[2] See J. Jewkes, D. Sawers and R. Stillerman, *op. cit.*, p. 214.

decision. Individuals undertake the low-cost and high-uncertainty activities, while firms undertake the high-cost and less-uncertain development activities.

The product cycle thesis can also throw some light on the research and development activities of large and small firms. In areas of rapid technological advance, many products will be in the first stage of the cycle. Here, the acquisition of technological competence is essential and large scale, marketing and development activities are not necessary. At this stage, the large firm's advantage may not be great, but as the technology matures scale becomes increasingly important and the advantages of the largest companies progressively become greater. This sort of explanation is consistent with developments in computers, scientific instruments and office equipment, although it cannot explain experience in more technologically stable sectors or in chemicals.

We have some statistics on research and development in small firms and these seem to confirm the observations that we have made.[1] A small firm is defined as a firm employing less than 200 people. In manufacturing, such firms are responsible for one-third of total employment, but for only 15% of the employment of qualified scientists and engineers and for 6% of the research and development financed by industry. Small firms conform roughly to the same pattern of research intensity that was observed for the whole of industry in Chapter 4. Small firms in chemicals and engineering (including vehicles) account for about 84% of research and development expenditure made by all small firms in manufacturing.

Most small firms spend very little on research and development. Two-thirds spent, in 1967, between £50 and £500 a year. Thus, as one would expect, small firms rely heavily on outside laboratories to do their research work. Small firms in electronics have 10% of employees in the industry, but employ 14% of the industry's qualified scientists and engineers. In the mechanical and electrical engineering industries, and in vehicles, however, the opposite pattern is shown. Their share of the employment of qualified scientists and engineers is less than their share of total employment. In electronics, large capital facilities are unnecessary and, as we have argued above, the expense required to develop an advanced technology is low relative to that necessary in the other branches of engineering.

RISK, UNCERTAINTY, AND THE APPRAISAL OF RESEARCH AND DEVELOPMENT PROJECTS

The presence of risk and uncertainty makes the appraisal of research

[1] J. Cox, *Scientific and Engineering Manpower and Research in Small Firms*, Committee of Inquiry on Small Firms: Research Report No. 2, London, 1971.

and development projects difficult and may influence the distribution of research and development expenditure between firms of varying sizes. The *ex ante* evaluation of research projects will be extremely difficult. In general it will be easier to estimate the returns to innovation than to estimate the returns to development, and easier, in turn, to estimate returns to development than those to research. In order to estimate the returns on a major piece of research, the firm has to guess the probability of the research yielding results worth developing. The cost of the research and of the development will be difficult to assess, as these are bound to take time. If development is successful, the costs of innovation, including investment in plant, and the returns in the form of future profits on this expenditure have to be estimated. Where the innovation produces a new product the task of estimating sales revenue and hence profits will be greatest. From case studies of innovation it seems that the time interval from the invention of a new process, to a product's first sales on a commercial basis, is on average (with considerable variation between firms and industries) ten years. Thus, the total interval between research which is aimed at a significant technological advance and profits will often be upwards of fifteen years.

The uncertainty decreases as one moves from basic research through development to innovation, but remains high at the innovation stage. This will be discussed in Chapter 6, but it is important to note here that the correlation between expected and actual returns to innovation are low. In a study in the U.K. this correlation was found to be 0·13, with over- and under-estimation of the probable yields being equally likely.[1] The greatest uncertainty will be in sectors where technological knowledge is changing rapidly, for there the possibility of competitive inventions and innovations has to be seriously considered. Yet, it is in precisely these areas where correct decision making is most important.[2] On the basis of some evidence, it seems that about half of research and development projects yield no commercially applicable results.

In these circumstances it is a heroic task for a firm to attempt an appraisal of research or development projects using numerical techniques. Although such attempts were made in the full flush of enthusiasm for discounted cash flow techniques in the 1960s, it is being increasingly realized that this method is too blunt an instru-

---

[1] C. F. Carter and B. R. Williams, *Investment in Innovation*, London, Oxford U.P., 1958, p. 90.

[2] It is important to distinguish between uncertainty and risk. Risks are events whose chances of occurring are known, i.e. the probability distribution is known. Where there is uncertainty, neither the events, nor the chances of them occurring, are known. Risk can be insured against; uncertainty cannot.

ment for the purpose of research expenditures. Partly this is because the pay-off—if any—of research, and some development, expenditures is likely to come, as we have explained, in the distant future. If the firm uses the same rate of discount in its appraisal of research expenditure as in the case of fixed investment, for example, returns in the distant future will be heavily discounted and will count for very little. Typically, firms use short pay-back periods in their appraisal, which only emphasizes the earlier conclusion.

A more important reason why numerical appraisals of research and development activities are of dubious value is that the numbers that are assigned to future flows of revenue and cost, and the probabilities given to various possible outcomes, must be largely arbitrary. Professor Shackle has devoted great effort to the study of the conditions of uncertainty in which investment is undertaken. This is not the place to summarize his results, but it is fair to say that our impression is that 'animal spirits' govern much innovatory investment.

Total expenditure on research and development is often decided by rule of thumb. In pharmaceuticals, it goes up when profits go down. Alternatively, a firm may decide its expenditure on the basis of a given percentage of turnover, or it may simply decide to keep its levels of activity more or less in line with those of its competitors; or expenditure may be dictated by fashion. Total expenditure can then be adjusted over the years in line with estimated *ex post* yields to research and development. However, returns to past research and development may be difficult to interpret for the purpose of deciding future expenditure.

Although total research expenditure can be decided in this way, there remains the problem of project selection. A discussion of the decision processes lies outside the scope of this book, but two points can be made.[1] First, an economic evaluation is useful, for it forces people to think clearly about the implications of any proposal. In such an evaluation, weights may be given to various factors, although it is misleading to end up with a simple numerical result. Secondly, all branches of a company should take part in the decision. The complete integration of research departments with the rest of the company has been emphasized by most studies as a necessary condition for successful innovation.

Although formal investment appraisals are not used to any great extent, this does not mean that an aversion to uncertainty or a preference for returns in the near, rather than the distant, future play no part in determining the scope or type of research and development undertaken. Thus, to return to our discussion of the relationship

[1] For a brief summary, see A. Pearson, 'Planning of Research and Development', *Long Range Planning*, 1972.

between the size of firm and research expenditures, it is possible to argue that the tendency for research and development to be concentrated in large firms can be explained through uncertainty. It is known that a high proportion of research projects come to nothing. The larger the number of projects undertaken by a firm, the smaller the chance of all failing. Further, research may lead to major breakthroughs which can only be developed by large firms, because there are substantial economies of scale in maintaining research and development activities. This is particularly true, as we have argued, in mature technologies. Similarly, it is sometimes suggested that diversified firms are most suited to undertake research. The reasoning behind this contention is that the results may be in a field different from that originally intended. The firm which is diversified will be able to make use of a higher percentage of unexpected results, so that the expected profitability of research expenditures will be higher for such firms. Tests of this hypothesis have not proved conclusive. Most big firms are diversified and research and development is important in furthering the objectives of such firms. This is discussed in the subsequent section.

It must be emphasized at this point that most applied research and development is not aimed at major technological advance, but at a variety of small changes to products and processes. The McGraw-Hill survey showed that, in 1961, 90% of firms expected to recoup their expenditure in less than six years from the start of the project. Thus, most research and development is devoted to modest improvements of a routine nature. The statistical evidence is backed up by qualitative work, both in the U.K. and in the U.S.A. Research and development devoted to major advance is concentrated in a few industries—aerospace, chemicals and electronics.

It is not clear whether firms' emphasis on short term projects represents a misallocation from the point of view of society. The implicit or explicit use of short pay-back periods may mean that potentially profitable projects are missed. On the other hand, if firms are not willing to undertake longer term projects, they clearly have a good reason for not doing so. Businessmen may be right. Certainly, aerospace could never have developed without government aid and who would dare to say that this development has represented a social optimum? As we have seen, however, acceptance of this argument is unlikely to affect expenditure on basic research, because such expenditures are more likely to be settled on some other basis. As far as development is concerned, the implicit use of high discount rates on routine development expenditure is not likely to lead to misallocation, because these expenditures will meet firms' investment criteria. Our conclusion is that modern management techniques may lead to under-investment in long term developments of major importance, especially when the financial commitment by a firm would be large. There is in these cases a presumption that some form of governmental support or action is necessary. This is what takes place, and its scale is described in Chapter 8.

RESEARCH AND DEVELOPMENT AND THE EXPANSION OF FIRMS

The annual reports of large companies are singularly uninformative documents. In these reports, however, firms are able to include those aspects of their activities that they wish to emphasize. An inspection of annual reports makes it clear that research and development is considered worthy of emphasis by some large companies but not by others. The reports of ICI, the Rank Organisation, Shell, Standard Telephones and Cables, and Sulzer, to name but a few, devote considerable space to their current research and development activities. In some cases, past technological achievements are emphasized. Sulzer, for example, gives a chronological list of inventions and innovations for which the firm has been responsible. In other reports the research and development department does not get a mention. Now much of this is simply an exercise in public relations. It is suggested that signs of spectacular research activity may help a company's stock market evaluation and that the emphasis is always on activities not results.[1] Generally it seems correct to take a less sceptical view. Research and development is concentrated in a few industries, and companies in these industries undertake these activities in order to further their objectives, notably the desire for expansion.

A firm can expand by diversification and/or by the acquisition of other firms. Growth by diversification can occur either through the development of new products or through entering existing markets which the firm had previously ignored. Before we consider the influence of research and technology on these two alternative directions of growth, it is useful to be clear about the immediate objectives of industrial research and development expenditures. A survey carried out in the U.S.A. in 1966 estimated that the main objectives of research and development expenditures were new product development in 45% of companies, product improvement in 41%, and new processes in 14%. What little information there is for the U.K. suggests that there is rather more emphasis here on new processes, although product research is the main objective of about two-thirds of firms. New products sometimes imply new production processes,

[1] G. Bannock, *The Juggernauts*, London, Weidenfeld, 1971, p. 179.

but more usually they can be produced by modifying existing processes.

In order to grow through diversification, a firm has to shift the demand curve for its products outwards to the right. We are here talking of the demand curve for all of the products of the firm—a sort of corporate demand curve.[1] The types of expenditure whose main object is to shift the demand curve in this way have been referred to as growth inducing expenditures. Important among such activities are advertising, marketing, and research and development. One direction of growth is by developing new products and the central role of research and development in furthering corporate objectives in this way is clear. To get the emphasis between research and development right, we must remember that new products in this sense need only be slight improvements in existing products, implying the importance of development rather than research expenditures. Research can be important in developing new products and may give a company a longer lasting lead than do trivial improvements. The new tyre developed by Dunlop that will remain inflated even when punctured is probably a case in point. Biological washing powders, however, although the outcome of research programmes, have not given the innovator a lasting lead because competitors had been engaged simultaneously in similar research.

Another form of diversification is expansion into new markets. Here the notion of a 'technological base' is important. A technological base of a firm exists where there are a group of productive activities in which certain materials, machines, skills, and processes are closely associated and complementary to one another.[2] A firm may have more than one technological base, and in such cases the bases will often be linked by common scientific and technological knowledge. Penrose and others have stressed the importance of a company having a strong technological base in any new markets it may enter. This is not to ignore the importance of marketing factors, and in some sectors of the economy, such as food, textiles and clothing, strength in marketing will be more important than technological competence. Research and development activities will strengthen a company's technological bases and will be capable of expanding them. In the latter case, research and development will more directly influence the direction of expansion. For example, the research departments of large brewing companies possessed a considerable knowledge of fermentation and moulds. The same sort of knowledge was required

[1] R. Marris, *The Economic Theory of Managerial Capitalism*, London, Macmillan, 1964.
[2] E. Penrose, *The Theory of the Growth of the Firm*, Oxford, Blackwell, 1960, ch. VII.

70

in the development of antibiotics and both Guinness and Schenley Distillers Co. were able to diversify into the rapidly expanding antibiotics industry after the Second World War.[1] Another notable example of companies diversifying from a technological base is the movement of the major oil-refining companies into plastics, chemicals and synthetic rubber. ICI expanded into textiles through the formation, with Courtaulds, of British Nylon Spinners in 1940. The new product and the new technique have become important forms of competition. More important—as the above examples illustrate—a company's potential competitors may come from outside the range of existing producers. Penrose saw the industrial research laboratory as 'the logical response of the individual firm to the challenge inherent in the Schumpeterian process of creative destruction.' This needs to be qualified, since we have seen that in many industries very little is spent on research or development. In the research intensive sectors it is clear, however, that research and technology are important factors in determining the rate and direction of a company's diversification.

Research and development also play an important part in determining the pattern of merging, which is the other principal method of expansion. The link between research and development, diversification and mergers has been confirmed by empirical studies.[2] Two main conclusions can be drawn from these studies. First, a majority of diversifying mergers takes place within a narrow industrial spectrum. Secondly, such diversification appears to be facilitated in industries which have high research expenditures and in which a high proportion of total employment is made up of technically qualified personnel. This also seems to hold true for conglomerates which, by definition, are located in several industries—but there is a tendency for them to have their major interests in two research intensive industries, chemicals and engineering.

INVENTIVE ACTIVITY AND MARKET STRUCTURE

There has been some study of the relationship between the market structure of an industry and the scale of inventive activity in that industry. For several reasons this is a difficult question to analyse and it may, in fact, not be a very meaningful question to ask.

Market structure, expenditure on research and development, and the scientific character of the industry are all closely related. This

[1] Guinness's antibiotic interests have now been sold off.
[2] These are surveyed by A. Wood, 'Diversification, Merger, and Research Expenditures: A Review of Empirical Studies', in: R. Marris and A. Wood (eds), *The Corporate Economy*, London, Macmillan, 1971.

makes it difficult, as in so much else, to identify the separate relationships. Much of what we are discussing is a closely linked series of complex interactions. We have already argued that the primary determinant of the profitability of research and development activity is the technological nature of the industry. In technologically advanced industries based on widely known science and technology, research and development expenditure is more likely to yield profitable results than elsewhere. The same factors also tend to lead—because, for example, they yield economies of scale—to oligopolistic or monopolistic structures. Thus, the electrical engineering industry spends a large amount on research and development relative to net output and it is dominated by a few large firms. Are we thus entitled to conclude that the oligopolistic nature of the industry favours inventive activity? The same applies to nationalized industries. In the U.K., steel, fuel (except for oil), rail and air transport, atomic energy and (in the service trades), health and the Post Office are run in various ways by the government. Are these large units, having centralized buying, research and development activities and investment, and highly developed management structures, likely to lead to more or less invention?

The question we are interested in is as follows. Will an industry in the private sector with a given technological base, undertake more or less research and development, if it is monopolistic, oligopolistic or competitive? Unfortunately we cannot experiment and vary the amount of competition, holding other things constant, so what we observe in practice is the combined effect of various influences.

It is difficult, then, to separate out the effect of market structure from that of firm size. If an industry dominated by three large firms spends heavily on research and development, is it because the firms are large or because there are only three of them? In this context, it becomes less and less meaningful to so tightly separate invention and innovation. The best measure from our present viewpoint of the merits of different forms of competition is the technological advances they yield. Empirically, technological advances are best studied through changes in productivity. However, these changes depend, not only on innovation, but also on the rate at which innovations are diffused. Diffusion rates may also be a function of the market structure, which makes it impossible to identify the effect of that market structure on invention. We shall discuss the diffusion of innovations later.

The evidence on the relationship between invention and market structure is conflicting and does not throw up any general rules. Some concentrated industries, such as petrochemicals, have been in the van of technological advance and have spent relatively large sums on research and development, while others, such as linoleum, have not. Nor have econometric studies come up with any very conclusive results.[1] Most applied economists who have studied the question lay emphasis upon international competition and emulation. This is important, but what is at issue is the interpretation of the facts, and in such a case the argument must rest partly on an *a priori* basis.

We shall therefore briefly outline some of the more pertinent points that have been made, while admitting to being sceptical of the importance of this question. We shall use a simple three-way classification of market structures—monopoly, oligopoly and competition.

The view that monopolists are uniquely suited to inventive activity dates from the writings of Schumpeter and the German and Austrian school of economists from which he came.[2] The factors favouring monopoly are three-fold. First, and most obviously, the monopolist will tend to have the greatest ability to finance research and development expenditures. Lenders of capital generally find it very difficult to assess the risks and prospects of research and development projects and are reluctant to lend money for such purposes. It thus follows that for research and development firms cannot depend on external financing and have to rely on internal financing. Small firms, especially 'young' firms, will tend to have small accumulated resources of undistributed profits and will be inclined to devote those that they do have to less risky projects, such as fixed capital expenditure. Government support of research programmes, and more recently of venture groups, have diminished the relative advantage of the monopolist in this respect.

Secondly, because of his control over the market, the monopolist will be more able than other firms to appropriate the results of his research and development expenditure. This is especially important, as we have seen, in the case of basic research and to a lesser extent in the case of applied research. Thirdly, it is sometimes argued that monopolistic firms will have the most highly trained and most skilled managers. This argument seems highly contentious and it would appear unwise to place much emphasis on it. Indeed, the opposite might well be the case. The factors working against monopoly in this respect are largely the mirror image of those in favour of other forms of competition, so we shall not duplicate them.

Two major points, however, can be made. It is argued that monopolists do not have the incentive generated by competition. But as

[1] See, e.g. R. Scherer, *op. cit.*
[2] Although it must be emphasized that Schumpeter was writing of innovation, not invention.

long as monopolists are aiming to maximize their growth, they will have the same incentive to undertake potentially profitable research and development as other firms. The argument only holds true, therefore, if monopolists opt for 'the quiet life'. Which leads us to the second point: in the whole of this argument what really matters is not so much the existing market structure but the ease of entry into the market. It can be objected that entry into a monopolistic industry, by definition, is difficult. Firms in other industries which are similar technologically to a monopoly may, however, gain results from their research expenditure that can be applied in the monopolistic industry. If they choose to exploit these results, they can bring in their own protection in the form of patents. Thus, entry to an apparently monopolistic market may be secured in this way.

The underlying theory of oligopoly tends to be somewhat unsatisfactory and there is a variety of models of oligopoly. It is not our purpose to review these, but the lack of agreement about how oligopolistic firms behave makes it difficult to deduce their attitude to research and development. We may, however, make the generalization that price competition under oligopoly tends to be relatively weak and that competition takes other forms. One such form is the introduction of new products. This is the essence of the argument that such firms will be induced to spend relatively large sums on research and development. It has to be admitted, however, that the aim of such research and development may largely be product differentiation rather than to develop new products in the strict sense of the term. The introduction of new products is only one form of non-price competition, and the reaction of a firm to a product innovation by a competitor may not be to spend more on research or development but to spend more on say, advertising.

In both competitive and oligopolistic industries, it can be argued that the potential market gains from research and development, or more correctly the subsequent innovations, are large since successful firms can capture the markets of their rivals. This is probably a more important influence in the case of competitive industries. This argument depends for its force on the ability of the successful firm to appropriate the results of its research and development. The more severe the competition, the more likely it is that other firms will be able to capture some of the results and adapt them for their own purposes. As we have argued earlier, patents give only partial protection.

It follows that the argument is an inconclusive one. Some factors favour one form of structure while others favour another. It can be seen that *a priori* reasoning does not yield very clear cut results in this case. Some factors favour one form of structure, others another.

We think that in the end one comes back to the technological nature of the industry as being the major determining factor of its scale of inventive activities. This is only one influence on the structure of an industry. It has been suggested that it is possible that economies of distribution, for example, may lead to a highly concentrated industry, while a larger number of smaller firms might be best suited—given the character of the industry—to undertake research and development.[1]

[1] R. Nelson, M. Peck and E. Kalachek, *op. cit.*, p. 72.

CHAPTER 6

Innovation

Innovation is the embodiment of an invention in the productive process and is, as such, a crucial step in economic change. Research and development activities have potentially positive effects on the output of goods and services, but it is not until a new process is actually undertaken, or a new product introduced, that this potential is realized. It is difficult in practice to identify exactly the beginning and end of the innovative process. In the same way, as we have seen, it is difficult to place the act of invention neatly between research and development. At the first stage, the line between development and innovation is not at all clear. Conceptually it is neat to think of development culminating with a blueprint of a plant to produce a new product, or to utilize a new process, which is then built and machinery installed. At this point innovation occurs. In practice, however, this is too simple a view. Once a new product is produced, or a new process put into use, faults will be identified by production departments or by consumers, and the subsequent improvements must strictly be viewed as development—yet they occur after innovation. Our clear definitions, then, hide a complex reality.

Not all of the ideas emanating from research and development departments lead to innovations and not all innovations are successful. Whether or not to innovate may seem a straightforward investment decision. There is great difficulty, however, in estimating a technologically uncertain future and there are serious problems in estimating the costs of production when new processes are involved. The RB211 engine and the Concorde aircraft are examples of cost estimates that were devastatingly incorrect. There are, in most cases, even more serious problems in estimating the revenue accruing from an innovation.

The risks involved in selling a new process or product can to some extent be reduced by carrying out product and market tests, in order to assess more clearly the chances of acceptance. It has been stated that in the U.S.A. about half of new products and processes fail in such tests. Innovation does not occur, yet many of the costs have been incurred. Acceptance of an idea on the basis of a market test is no guarantee of success, as is witnessed by the fact that less than half of new products or processes that passed market and acceptance tests became commercial successes.

Because of the ambiguities involved in precisely dating invention and innovation, it is difficult to measure the lag between invention and innovation. Where the invention is of a trivial or routine nature —as most are—such lags will be short. This is not so in the case of significant advances, and it is in these cases that the problems of identifying dates of invention and innovation are greatest. Enôs has provided data for thirty-five major product and process innovations.[1] His criterion for inclusion in his sample was simply that it was possible to date the invention and innovation with reasonable accuracy. His results show that the average interval between invention and innovation is 13·6 years. The standard deviation is 16·3 years, and so the distribution appears far from normal. Although it is difficult to draw strong conclusions from such a sample, it appears that mechanical innovations required the shortest time interval and that the time-interval appears to be shorter when the same firm is responsible for both the invention and innovation. Further studies suggest that the average time interval may be shorter now than at the beginning of the century.[2] The safest statement, however, seems to be that the interval varies widely, even within industries, and that no clear rule emerges.

In many cases of major advances the absence of complementary conditions or impropitious factor prices may impede innovation. The cotton picker provides a good example of such obstacles. A labour saving device is unlikely to be adopted quickly when labour is abundant and capital is scarce. The cotton picker was invented in 1889, yet it was fifty-nine years before innovation took place, in 1948. In the twenty years subsequent to invention, Campbell—the inventor—took models for testing into the cotton fields of the American South. Development was severely hindered by a lack of finance and by poor facilities for carrying out mechanical work. Following Campbell's death in 1922, the International Harvester Co. took over the patents. The cotton picker is a labour saving device, and with the level of unemployment and wages prevailing in the 1930s there was little incentive to devote many resources to its

[1] J. Enôs, 'Invention and Innovation in the Petroleum Refining Industry', In: *The Rate and Direction of Inventive Activity*, Princeton, Princeton University Press, 1962.
[2] E. Mansfield, 'Determinants of the Speed of Application of New Technology', Paper read to the Conference of the International Economics Association, 1971.

development. Production on a small scale started, in 1942, when labour grew scarce, but it was not until 1948 that its use was widespread enough to say that innovation had occurred.

In determining the efficiency and profitability of an innovation, the crucial lag is not that between invention and innovation, but rather between the decision to innovate and innovation. Such lags are usually referred to as lead times and we shall discuss below the factors influencing lead times.

Innovation is normally the most costly part of the research, development, and innovation process. Terylene was invented in a small laboratory with low costs, but subsequently cost ICI £4 million in development costs. The new plant for commercial production of Terylene cost the company £15 million. Innovation is the *embodiment* of technical change in a new plant and machinery, and this is one reason for the high costs. A second reason is that the launching of a new or improved product is usually accompanied by a considerable marketing effort. In the U.S.A., the average division of launching costs is: 5–10% research; 10–20% development; and 70–85% innovation costs. Such averages conceal considerable differences in relative costs as between industries and products. Many innovations have no research costs, and where the construction of prototypes or pilot plants is necessary the share of development rises, as such costs are conventionally classified as development. In chemical process plants, the pilot plant is an essential stage in the innovative process, because often it is not possible to predict large scale catalytic reactions from laboratory scale work. Thus, development may typically account for up to 30% of launching costs in this industry.

Innovation is the crucial link between research and development activity, and the sale of new products, or of products produced using new processes. It is therefore not surprising that the conditions under which efficient and successful innovation can occur have been the subject of considerable study. In the next section we discuss the main results of such work.

SUCCESSFUL INNOVATION

The conclusion that is supported by virtually all the evidence is that innovation is a two-sided activity. On the one hand, is the need for technical expertise; on the other, the need for a successful marketing approach (to recognize market needs) before the innovation can be sold. The successful innovators are those who 'marry' these two facets of innovation, and who, in fact, link innovation closely with all of the organization's activities. It is essential to bear these interactions in mind as we discuss, in turn, various influences on the success or

78

failure of an innovation. The importance of management is obvious, since it is management's task to obtain such co-ordination and it is thus useful to leave a discussion of management until the end.

Innovations are based on inventions or, more generally, on ideas. The Manchester study of innovations that won Queen's Awards to Industry for technological innovation found that of the 158 important 'ideas' that were utilized in 51 innovations, one-third emanated within the firm and two-thirds from other sources.[1] We have dealt with sources internal to the firm in Chapter 4 and so here we concentrate on external sources. For a firm to take advantage of research and development results from elsewhere, it has to have good communications with the scientific and technical community at large. In addition it must be able to select the most promising results and adapt them to its own circumstances. Freeman found that although large firms claimed to be responsible for much innovation in chemical process plant in general, major innovations were 'the result of assimilating and stimulating scientific and technical advances in a number of different places—universities, government laboratories, contractors, consultants and component makers'.[2] The Sussex study of innovation similarly confirmed the importance of specialized communication with the scientific and technological community. This project is especially interesting because it attempts to see if there are any characteristics which occur more often in failures than in successes—and vice versa.[3] The methodology of the research project is to 'pair' successful and unsuccessful innovations of similar products and processes. This is possible usually, because several firms attempt the same innovation in the world market at roughly the same time. This confirms the experience of scientists of the process of multiple-discovery. It suggests that in technology, as in science, there is a 'frontier' of knowledge which several search parties are reaching at the same time. The Sussex team studied fifty-eight attempted innovations in the chemical and scientific instrument industries. The pairs were defined in market rather than technical terms, as were the meanings of 'success' and 'failure'. That is to say, a *failure* was defined as an innovation that failed to establish a market, or failed to make a profit, or failed to do either. The opposite criteria defined a *success*. Problems of 'semi-failures' were avoided by concentrating on clear-cut successes and failures. As life is full of 'half-failures', it is possible that some interesting cases were omitted

[1] J. Langrish, *et al.*, *Wealth from Knowledge*, London, Macmillan, 1972, p. 78.
[2] C. Freeman, 'Chemical Process Plant: Innovation and the World Market', *National Institute Economic Review*, 1968.
[3] C. Freeman, 'A Study of Success and Failure in Industrial Innovation', Paper read to the Conference of the International Economics Association, 1971.

from the study. Specialized communication was a characteristic associated with successful innovation. Carter and Williams put forward as two of the characteristics of the 'technically progressive' firm, a high quality of incoming information and the deliberate surveying of this information.[1] They found that backward firms often fail to hear of an idea until several years after it is made known. Freeman quotes the example of a chemical firm in the U.S.A. working on the development problems of heat exchanges and distillation. These difficulties had in fact been solved several years earlier and, consequently, the firm would have saved itself time and money merely by sifting the contents of high quality technical journals. Alternatively, an outside contractor could have brought it to their notice, if consulted. This illustration serves to emphasize the point made earlier that for firms who do not wish to have, or are not large enough to have, a sizable research and development department, the employment of a few qualified scientists and engineers can yield dividends by screening information. We would note here that the Sussex study found that the size of the research and development department was not associated with success or failure in innovation. There was a similarly great variation in the number of qualified scientists and engineers employed in different firms, but this number was not related to success or failure.

A successful marketing organization has been emphasized in most work as being a key factor in successful innovation. There are various aspects to this. The first, chronologically, is the perception of a market need and an understanding of user requirements. We have already discussed the relative importance of technology push and market pull factors, and we have seen from the published evidence that market-pull factors appear to have been dominant in a majority of cases. Often, however, there are too many complications to make such a clear distinction. There are examples of innovations that have been specifically market based; that is to say, in which market research has defined a need which the research and development department has subsequently attempted to meet. Hawker Siddeley have tended to favour this approach. Where innovation stems from unforeseen technological changes, market influences are negligible and there is some evidence that market forces are more important in engineering where advance is relatively predictable. Where marketing does not guide innovation it remains crucial, for the products of innovation have to be sold. Users of new products have to be 'educated', publicity has to be undertaken, and the whole range of marketing activities are probably more important in the selling of new,

[1] C. Carter and B. Williams, *Industry and Technical Progress*, London, Oxford U.P., 1957.

80

rather than existing, products. Marketing must be linked with technical expertise, but the precise form the linkage takes will vary widely.

There seems to be no clear link between the size of firm and innovation. Most of the points made in our discussion of the relationship between the size of firm and inventive activity are appropriate here and we shall not repeat them. In the research project into success and failure in innovation, the size of firm had no pervasive effect. As the authors point out, this should not be interpreted as implying that the size of firm has absolutely no effect, because, whether innovation occurs at all may be connected with the size of firm. In the chemicals industry, only four innovations occurred in firms employing fewer than 1,000 people, but in scientific instruments over half the innovations took place in such firms. This observation lends emphasis to the point made earlier that it is the character of the industry which determines whether or not firm size is important in affecting the propensity to innovate.

Mansfield has examined the relationship between firm size and innovation, relating the market share of the four largest firms in each of three industries to their share of the innovations undertaken in each industry.[1] This is inevitably a crude exercise, because it is only possible to make a subjective evaluation of the importance of each innovation. The results showed that in the coal and petroleum industries the share of the four largest firms in innovative activity exceeded their market share, but that the opposite was true in the steel industry. One must be careful in interpreting these results, for Mansfield suggests that there is little evidence to support the notion that large *individual* firms carried out a greater number of innovations relative to their size than did small firms. Large firms were, of course, responsible for the greatest absolute number of innovations.

Finally, we briefly consider the management of innovations. We shall discuss two aspects of the role of management. First, the importance of 'key individuals' in the innovative process, and secondly the organizational structure that may be best suited to innovating firms.

Some writers have emphasized the importance of the presence of one individual in an organization who is totally dedicated and committed to pushing through an innovation. This individual may be in a research department, but will usually have executive authority; he may run the organization. A major innovation will often run into difficulties, and to overcome these additional resources will be needed. Problems can occur at any stage in the process, from research onwards, and it is at these times that the work needs a 'champion' to

[1] E. Mansfield, 'Size of Firm, Market Structure and Innovation', *Journal of Political Economy*, 1963.

argue the case and obtain the resources. Langrish and his colleagues cite many examples of innovations where the support of one or a few individuals was crucial. Work on reactive dyes by ICI is a good example. Reactive dyes are dye-stuffs which react with cellulosic fibres to give bright, colour-fast shades. Two individuals championed the project in the post-war years and they 'were able to ginger the whole development machinery into an unusual activity'.[1] The Manchester study found, in fact, that the presence of an outstanding individual was the most important of all those factors which favoured successful innovation. In 40% of all the innovations analysed the role of one or two individuals was crucial. The Sussex research workers did not specifically analyse the roles of individuals, but they did examine the characteristics of those who managed innovations. There was some tendency for successful managers of innovation to be older, have greater status, and to exercise greater power within the firm than those who were unsuccessful. This may be important in determining the ability of a manager to marshal resources into specific project teams. Perhaps it implies a greater willingness or ability to accept risks. The qualifications of the person responsible within the management structure for the supervision of a project does not, incidentally, seem to vary systematically with success or failure in innovation. In the Manchester study, too, the educational background of men identified as key individuals varied widely and the possession of scientific or technological qualifications did not seem important.

A radical innovation will affect most branches of a company from research and development through design to changes in production processes—and perhaps investment in new plants, which may imply some change in the skill requirements of various tasks. To be successful, such changes on the production side have to be matched by marketing and selling efforts. Thus it is wrong to see invention and innovation as being the sole concern of research and development departments. The whole organization is affected. Yet the people in each part of the organization will tend to have different attitudes, values and vocabularies. The problems encountered in incorporating scientists into an industrial organization have been well documented.[2] It seems clear that the quality of management will be a crucial factor in determining the degree of success of an innovation.

Firms outside the research intensive group of industries will be to some extent sheltered from the problems of organizing innovation, and it is suggested that different management structures will be most

[1] J. Langrish, et al., op. cit., p. 18. See also pp. 308–19.
[2] E.g. see, S. Box and S. Cotgrove, 'Scientific Identity, Occupational Selection and Role Strain', British Journal of Sociology, 1966.

appropriate in different types of firms. There are many dimensions to the optimum structure, and here we will simply look at the distinction made between 'organic' and 'mechanistic' systems of management.[1] Burns and Stalker have argued that not only is a firm's managerial system affected by the nature of the production process, but also by the extent to which the process is stable or unstable. The mechanistic system is appropriate under stable conditions and roughly corresponds to the concept of a bureaucracy. Tasks are broken down into well-defined separate specialist functions, each of which is largely pursued independently. The structure of control, communication and authority is highly hierarchical; that is, the interaction between members of the organization is vertical with little horizontal interaction (except at the highest level) between the different parts of the organization. Of the other features of the mechanistic system we should mention the emphasis on localized, as opposed to cosmopolitan, knowledge, experience and skill. Burns and Stalker suggest that such an organizational structure is perfectly rational and appropriate under fairly static conditions and in firms whose environment tends not to be subject to rapid change.

On the other hand, the 'organic' firm is appropriate to changing conditions, which give rise constantly to fresh problems and unforeseen requirements for action—which cannot be broken down or distributed automatically in a way arising from the functional rules defined within a hierarchical structure. Organic managerial systems have the following characteristics: individual tasks are defined with respect to the total situation of the enterprise and are constantly redefined as that situation changes; communication and interaction is lateral, rather than vertical, and this facilitates innovation which, as we have emphasized, has implications for many of a firm's activities; and teamwork is emphasized. Burns and Stalker suggest that in such organizations the individual is more committed to the well-being of the enterprise, and to its expansion. Such systems are stratified, but not in the same way as are mechanistic systems: 'Authority is taken by whoever shows himself most informed and capable, i.e., the "best authority".'

It must be emphasized that the above cases are extreme, and that elements from both will be present in most companies. Technologically dynamic firms are best served by relatively organic managerial systems. It is apparent, however, that it will be easiest for small and medium sized firms to adopt such a structure, but that as firms grow there will be an increasing tendency for the organization to become bureaucratic. To use a different terminology, the organic system is

[1] T. Burns and G. Stalker, *The Management of Innovation*, London, Tavistock, 1961.

entrepreneur based, while the mechanistic system is management based. As firms grow, the sheer complexity and scale of their operations force them to reorganize themselves into divisions and departments and to become more management based. This may militate against the flexibility and the co-ordination needed in major innovative projects. It is possible that here may lie part of the explanation of the observed failure of large firms to account for a disproportional share of innovations, despite the apparent advantage they have in finance and the scale of production and marketing.

The problem of co-ordination in large organizations is not, of course, peculiar to innovative activity and many strategies to overcome managerial diseconomies are open to firms. One method that has been used in the context of innovation, notably by du Pont—a company noted for its success in this field—is to create a system of venture management. Essentially, this involves the separation of radical innovation from the main business, which effectively means that a small firm environment is created. This policy has apparently been pursued with some success by du Pont, although at some stage the small group must integrate with the whole organization.

The managerial difficulties which may be faced (especially by large companies) in innovating, probably serve to emphasize the importance of key individuals in the innovative process. We have mentioned the fact that the academic qualifications of such people do not seem to be very important, and it is not clear whether it is advantageous for management generally to hold scientific qualifications. Carter and Williams observed a slight tendency for technically progressive firms to have one or more board members who are scientists, and for unprogressive firms to have no scientists on the board. In research intensive industries this tendency was much stronger.

In examining the characteristics of firms which appear to be positively related to success in innovation, it becomes clear that many characteristics are those which one would associate with a generally successful firm. Although we have looked at management qualities and structures which are specially suited to innovations, it seems fairly clear that the ethos of good management will affect the efficiency with which all of a firm's activities are conducted. Thus, Carter and Williams in their survey of invention and innovation in industry in the U.K. concluded that 'the firm which is good in applying science and technology is also of good "general quality" '.[1]

One way in which the advantages of efficiency in innovation is manifested is in relatively short lead times—i.e. the time-interval between the decision to innovate and innovation. The firm with the shortest lead time will normally have the goods available to sell

[1] C. Carter and B. Williams, op. cit., p. 184.

earlier than its competitors. There is evidence to suggest that companies in the U.S.A. have shorter lead times than U.K. companies. In electronic capital goods and aircraft, the difference in lead times has been put at about one year. This difference has sometimes been enough to enable firms in the U.S.A. to start innovation later than U.K. competitors and yet be in a position to market goods first.[1]

[1] *Technological Innovation in Britain,* London, HMSO, 1963.

CHAPTER 7

The Diffusion of Innovations

So far, we have taken the story to the point where one firm innovates. For technical change to have any significant impact on productivity and output the process innovation has to be adopted by other firms, and product innovations must be emulated by other firms or the product has to be adopted by a large number of consumers. The questions we now have to consider are: how does the use of a new process, or the production of a new good, spread—and what will determine the rate of this process of diffusion?

TECHNICAL CHANGE AND INVESTMENT

We start by looking at the production of new goods or the use of new processes by firms.[1] In virtually all cases this will involve firms in investment, because new plant and equipment will be needed. In other words, the technical change has to be embodied in capital goods. An understanding of the embodiment process is essential in analysing the rate of diffusion of innovations and, subsequently, the effect of technical change on the productivity growth of certain industries, and on economic growth in general.

We shall restrict our discussion initially to *process* innovations, and to those which have to be embodied in new plant and equipment. This investment has to occur for the innovation to spread, and it may represent either the replacement of existing machines or a new addition to capacity. We make the following simplifying assumptions:

1. It is possible to associate a price with the output of the new machine (process). In practice, it is often not possible to do so, because a machine will usually produce one component of a product and the firm can only put a price (and hence a profit margin) on the completed product.
2. There is full capacity utilization.

[1] The approach in this section follows that of W. Salter, *Productivity and Technical Change* (2nd edn), Cambridge, Cambridge University Press, 1969, ch. 4.

86

3. The industry is reasonably competitive in the sense that profits greatly in excess of normal will be competed away.
4. Process innovation has occurred at a fairly continuous—but not necessarily steady—rate in the past.
5. We can leave out of the analysis the scrap value, or the resale value, of machines.

Investment has occurred in the past, and so the industry's stock of the machines will consist of machines of different vintages. Since innovation is assumed to have occurred continuously, the machines of different vintages will have different operating costs. We can depict the industry's stock of machines and their associated operating costs as in Figure 7.1.

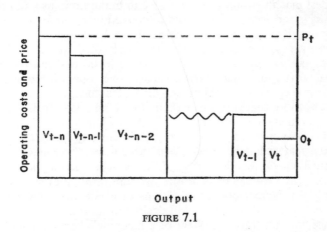

Output

FIGURE 7.1

The dimensions of the block V_t, in Figure 7.1, show on the horizontal axis the output produced with machines of the most recent vintage, and on the vertical axis the operating costs of these machines. The block V_{t-1} shows the output produced by the previous vintage, and the associated operating costs, and so on. The left-hand block refers to the oldest machines still in use. The blocks vary in width, reflecting varying amounts of investment in the past. Machines of any given vintage have lower operating costs than those of a previous vintage for two reasons. First, the older machines will have mechanically deteriorated to a greater extent, will need more maintenance, and may produce material that has to be wasted. Secondly, the more recent machines will be technically superior because they embody more recent techniques.

Now let us introduce the price of the product into the picture.

Under our assumption of a competitive industry, the price will be such that current investment yields a rate of profit that is in some sense normal. This rate of profit will tend to differ between industries for a variety of reasons, including differences in risk between industry. If new investment yielded a supernormal rate of return, then existing firms would have an incentive to invest more and perhaps new firms would enter the industry. As a result output would expand. Expansion would cause the price to fall to the point where the rate of profit became normal. Obviously this adjustment process may take some time to achieve, but it will take place so long as competitive conditions prevail. In Figure 7.1, the price P_t denotes the price that gives a surplus over operating costs on new machines $(P_t - O_t)$, such as to yield a normal rate of profit. This price at the same time determines the oldest machines that it is profitable to maintain in use. In economics—as in theology, as we should be constantly reminded—bygones are forever bygones. Once machines have been installed the only costs relevant are operating costs. Capital costs are relevant only with respect to decisions as to whether to instal new machines. As long as existing machines earn a surplus over operating costs, they are worth keeping in use. Thus, the oldest machines that will be kept going are those that just cover their operating costs. In Figure 7.1, this will be machines of vintage V_{t-n}. A machine will therefore earn a surplus over operating costs when it is first installed and this surplus (or quasi-rent) will decline over its lifetime until it becomes negative. The machine will then be scrapped. Thus, when making investment decisions, the firm has to take into account (among other matters), not only the current operating surplus of a new machine, but also the rate at which this surplus will decline in future.

Hence, we can trace the effect of a machine's becoming available which is superior to those of vintage V_t. The new machines will be of vintage V_{t+1}. We show the operating costs of these and trace out the effect of the innovation in Figure 7.2.

The new machines have lower operating costs of O_{t+1}. It does not automatically follow that they are worth installing. If they had the same capital costs as machines of vintage V_t, they would be worth installing, by definition, as long as price remained at P_t, because machines of vintage V_t have been installed up to the point where their present surplus, and expected future surpluses, over operating costs yield a normal return on investment. The new machines have lower operating costs and, thus, if they cost the same amount, must yield a supernormal rate of profit. Even this, of course, assumes that entrepreneurs have complete knowledge of the costs and performance of the new machines. As we shall see this may be an obstacle in the diffusion process. Leaving this aside for the moment, it does not automatically follow that innovation is worth while. Let us assume that the present surplus $P_t - O_{t+1}$ of the new machines is enough, given the capital costs, to yield super-normal rates of return on investment. As the new machines are installed, output will expand and price will fall until the yield on machines of vintage V_{t+1} is normal. Let that price be P_{t+1}. At this lower price, some of the older machines (in Fig. 7.2 those of vintage V_{t-n}) will no longer cover their operating costs and will be scrapped. The oldest machines used by the industry will now be those of vintage V_{t-n-1}. If no further development of machines were to occur, machines of vintage V_{t+1} would continue to be installed as the operating costs of the oldest vintages increased, because of deterioration, to the point where their price failed to cover operating costs.

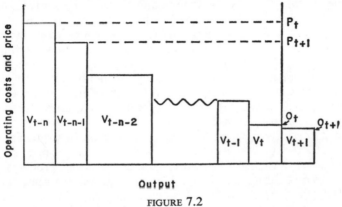

Output

FIGURE 7.2

We thus get the picture of continuing change in the industry's stock of machines. As new machines are developed they are introduced and the oldest machines are scrapped. At any one time the stock of machines will consist of a spectrum of vintages. Only a part of the output of the industry will be produced on the newest machines, or the most technically superior machines. It is clear, and this must be emphasized, that a failure to use the most up-to-date machines is not at all irrational. As long as older machines yield a surplus over operating costs, a sensible firm will continue to use them, rather than scrap them and replace them with the most recent machines. Thus, the productivity of a whole industry will always lag behind the productivity of 'best practice plants', or those plants using the most up-to-date techniques. As an example, Salter cites the data given in Table 7.1.

It can be seen from Table 7.1 that, typically, the average produc-

TABLE 7.1. *Productivity in the U.S.A. Blast-furnace Industry*

Gross tons of pig-iron produced per man-hour

	Best practice plants	Industry average
1921	0·428	0·178
1923	0·462	0·213
1925	0·512	0·285
1926	0·573	0·296

Source: W. Salter, *op. cit.*, p. 6.

tivity in the industry was about a half of productivity in the best-practice plants (the plants of the most recent vintage).

The model of the replacement process, outlined above, is a fairly simple one which abstracted from a number of complications. Most of the assumptions can be relaxed without altering the substance of the argument, and it is not necessary for our purposes to examine the detailed effects, except where they represent 'frictions', acting to prevent, or hinder, the adjustment process.[1]

There is one assumption that we must explicitly relax. It was assumed that technical change takes the form of new processes (i.e. better ways of producing existing products). We know, however, that in the majority of cases technical change takes the form of new products or improvements to existing products. In principle, this does not alter the operation of the model. This is because, as new machines are installed to produce new or improved products, the surpluses on existing machines will be reduced and the same sort of process will operate as before. It should be noted, however, that improvements to new products often entail only trivial changes to existing production methods. In these cases, this analysis does not apply with any force and such cases may be best considered as examples of disembodied technical change. New and improved products do complicate an analysis of the effects of technical change, since they involve quality changes which are extremely difficult to incorporate in conventional measures of output (see Ch. 10).

THE RATE OF DIFFUSION OF INNOVATIONS

Once a new technique has been adopted, the speed at which other firms adopt, or the speed at which consumers adopt, a new product differs widely. In this section we discuss what is known of the rate of diffusion or imitation. In the subsequent section, the sort of factors operating to influence the rate of diffusion will be discussed. We have

[1] See W. Salter, *op. cit.*, ch. 7.

90

to keep distinct the time pattern of adoption and the speed at which the process operates. We consider the time pattern first.

Most, but not all, of the empirical evidence suggests that the adoption of an innovation follows a bell-shaped, or normal, distribution curve. When plotted cumulatively to show the number of firms or consumers that have adopted an innovation in any given year, this distribution will yield an 'S'-shaped curve.

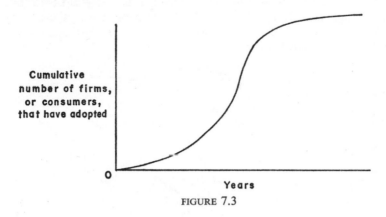

FIGURE 7.3

Some sort of 'S'-shaped distribution—but not necessarily that derived from a normal distribution—seems to summarize the spread of most new processes and products. There are two reasons for expecting such distribution to occur, and to avoid constant duplication of references to firms and consumers we shall discuss these reasons with reference to a process innovation. (Most of the argument applies equally to product innovations.)

First, the diffusion process is a learning process. Potential users have initially to become aware of the process and then attempt to evaluate it; subsequently, they may use it on a trial basis. Each stage is part of a learning process. Information has to be disseminated, and as the process is adopted by other firms, or by the firm on an experimental basis, this information becomes more reliable. Hitherto unforeseen snags will be overcome, which in turn reduces the risk. Psychologist's learning curves are normal, and the concept of the individual's learning curve can be extended to a group where experience with an innovation increases as each successive firm adopts the new process.[1] Therefore, the distribution of firms adopting an innovation might be expected to yield a normal curve.

Secondly, there is an interaction effect. When few firms have

[1] E. Rogers, *Diffusion of Innovations*, New York, Collier-Macmillan, 1962.

adopted an innovation, there is a small number of 'innovators' who can generate information on the process and from whom the idea can spread. At this point diffusion rates are low. As the number of users increases the 'information base' widens, and since there is still a large number of firms who have not adopted the new process the diffusion rate increases. As the proportion of users becomes large, however, the number of potential users still remaining becomes small. The remaining firms will necessarily tend to be those most resistant to change, and the increase in the cumulative number of firms that have adopted the new process will slow down. Such a process will yield an 'S'-shaped curve.[1]

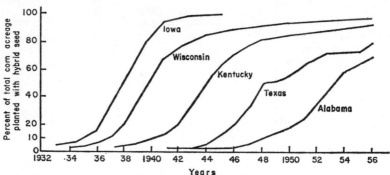

FIGURE 7.4. Rate of Diffusion of Hybrid Corn

Source: Z. Griliches, 'Hybrid Corn: An Exploration in the Economics of Technical Change,' *Econometrica*, 1957, p. 502.

Griliches's study (Fig. 7.4) of the spread of hybrid corn was the first formal study of diffusion rates. Hybrid corn was the invention of a method of propagation of the best corn for specific areas. Since it was not immediately applicable everywhere, it was possible for Griliches to study the adoption rate in different states in the U.S.A. There were, in fact, significant differences between states in the rate at which hybrid corn was adopted.

Griliches fitted logistic growth curves to his data. The logistic growth curve has the form:

$$P = \frac{K}{1 + \exp\{-(a+bt)\}}$$

where, in this case, P is the percentage of acreage planted with hybrid corn, K is the equilibrium value, and t is time. The parameters a and b can be estimated by least-squares from the linear transform of the equation: a is the intercept term, positioning the curve on the

[1] This is analogous to the changing rates at which an infectious disease spreads.

horizontal axis, and *b* gives the rate of diffusion. The parameters that were derived from the curves for different states showed wide variations. We shall return to these, and to the explanation of the differences, later in this chapter. For the moment we will describe other studies of the pattern of diffusion.

Mansfield studied the rate of diffusion of twelve innovations in four industries—coal, iron and steel, brewing, and railroads.[1] Small firms were excluded from the analysis, but for medium sized and large firms the spread of the innovations over time in most cases approximated to some sort of 'S'-shaped curve. Mansfield suggested, in fact, that a logistic curve best explains the spread of innovations.

For European countries, the most comprehensive study is that undertaken by the National Institute for Economic and Social Research. Their results confirm that an 'S'-shaped curve—but not the logistic form—best summarizes the spread of the ten process innovations that they examined.[2] 'S'-shaped growth patterns have also been observed for three innovations in the Lancashire textile industry.[3]

So far, we have looked at the spread of innovations among farmers and among firms. The diffusion of consumer goods is also of interest, for where product innovations are of this sort it is the rate of adoption of the new product by consumers that matters. Here the rate of acceptance by consumers affects the rate at which new goods are produced. The spread of some consumer-durable goods in the U.K. is shown in Figure 7.5.

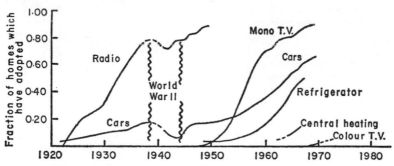

FIGURE 7.5 Adoption of Various Items by U.K. Households

Source: I. Hendry, 'The Three Parameter Approach to Long Range Forecasting,' *Long Range Planning*, 1972.

[1] E. Mansfield, *Industrial Research and Technological Innovation: an Econometric Analysis*, Harlow, Longman, 1969.

[2] G. Ray, 'The Diffusion of New Technology', *National Institute Economic Review*, 1970.

[3] J. Metcalfe, 'Diffusion of Innovation in the Lancashire Textile Industry' *Manchester School*, 1970.

There is not enough data to be clear about the rate of diffusion of central heating and colour television, but for the other products the pattern is very similar to that observed in the case of process innovations. It is interesting to note the interruptions to the growth curves for radio and cars caused by the Second World War.

The precise form of the diffusion curve is important for forecasting purposes. In this context, however, we are mainly concerned with the use of 'S'-shaped curves to summarize the diffusion process and we shall not discuss the various growth curves that may be used. As Griliches has written: 'In this work the growth curves serve as a summary device, perhaps somewhat more sophisticated than a simple average, but which should be treated in the same spirit.'

DETERMINANTS OF THE RATE OF DIFFUSION OF INNOVATIONS

Although the shape of the diffusion curve of many innovations appears to be 'S'-shaped, there are great differences in the speed at which innovations are diffused and thus in the length of the diffusion process. Differences in the diffusion of six techniques in the U.K. are shown in Table 7.2.

TABLE 7.2. *Diffusion of New Techniques: U.K.*

Innovation	Percentage of Output produced with New Technique	Years from Innovation*
Oxygen steel	20	5
Continuous casting of steel	6	1
Special presses in paper-making	10	3
Shuttleless loom	2	6
Automatic transfer lines for motor-car engines	30	10
Gibberellic acid used in malting	50	4

Source: G. Ray, *op. cit.*, p. 81.
* The years date from the first use of each technique in the U.K. and not from the date the technique was first used.

There are very marked differences in the speed at which these ~~ innovations are being adopted. The use of gibberellic acid in ~~ speeds up the malting process, has spread rapidly. process was first used in the U.K., 50% of malt is way. At the other extreme, it has taken six ton cloth to be produced on shuttleless looms. s there are wide variations in the rate of diffusion

94

between firms. For example, in the U.S.A. railroad industry, it took 20% of firms four years to increase their stock of diesel locomotives from 10% to 90% of their total locomotive stock, whereas 10% of firms took over fourteen years to achieve the same usage.[1]

We now examine the major factors which appear to affect the diffusion rate, drawing on the simple model of the adjustment process outlined in the first section of this chapter. The speed at which an innovation is accepted depends, first, on the characteristics of potential users of the innovation and, secondly, on the characteristics of the innovation itself. First, we consider how the characteristics of potential users affect the diffusion rate. The potential users of process innovations will be firms or farmers. We have seen that product innovations are quantitatively more important; and here the potential users will include consumers as well as firms and farmers. A

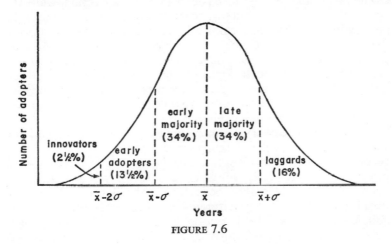

FIGURE 7.6

useful framework within which to categorize users has been provided by Rogers.[2] We noted earlier that the adoption of an innovation appears approximately to follow a normal distribution curve. Rogers uses this distribution to categorize adopters.

The normal distribution curve can be divided, as shown in Figure 7.6. Thus: 34% of all individuals will lie between the mean and mean less one standard deviation; 13½% between the mean less one standard deviation and the mean less two standard deviations; and so on. These groups are then labelled as in the diagram. The groups have

---

[1] E. Mansfield, 'Intra-firm Rates of Diffusion of an Innovation', *Review of Economics and Statistics*, 1963.
[2] E. Rogers, *op. cit.*

the following characteristics which we can broadly apply to firms buying new producer goods, or using new processes, or to consumers buying new products.

Innovators are venturesome and eager to try out new ideas. They have 'cosmopolitan' relationships—in the case of consumers, relationships will be social, and among firms the relationships will be with other firms, with suppliers, and with the scientific community. Innovators will generally have the financial resources necessary to bear any losses that may occur from time to time.

Early adopters evaluate innovations and adopt them if they seem profitable. Adopters are usually an integrated part of their social community and act as opinion leaders. In this way they probably have more influence on others than do innovators, who may be too atypical for others to identify with them.

The *early majority* tend to be deliberate in their action, while the *late majority* are always initially sceptical about an innovation. The latter tend to adopt an innovation when it has diffused to such an extent that its adoption is an economic necessity or, in the case of consumer goods, when the weight of public opinion testifies to the product's merit. Finally, there are the *laggards*—highly localized and traditionalists—whose decisions are often made with reference to the experience of a previous generation. By the time laggards adopt an innovation, it will often have been superseded.

The results of earlier research studies (largely sociological but some economic) aimed at defining the characteristics of the different types, are reviewed by Rogers. The groups can be summarized briefly as follows. Early adopters tend to be younger than late adopters, and to have higher social status and a higher level of educational attainment. In agriculture, it has been observed that early adopters tend to specialize in one or a few crops. Early adopters have several characteristics related to communication, which is probably very important in the context of the diffusion of innovations within industry. Early adopters rely to a greater extent on impersonal sources of information; their sources are wide and they have *more* sources of information. Generally, they use sources that are in close contact with the origin of new ideas. Thus, studies of the diffusion of hybrid corn have shown that early adopters tended to be those farmers with an above average level of educational attainment who technical journals.

In Chapter 6, we described the characteristics which seem to be associated with firms that have been successful in innovation, using that term in its strict sense to mean the first to adopt a new process or product. It seems that the characteristics of these firms generally can be applied also to innovators (as described in Fig. 7.6) and to early adopters, and so we shall not repeat them here. Such firms can be described as 'technically progressive', or as firms which are 'keeping close to the best which would reasonably be achieved in the application of science and technology'.[1] Communication and an openness to new ideas have been noted as features favouring early adoption of innovations, and we noted earlier that these will be characteristics of progressive firms.

The progressive firm takes a wide range of authoritative technical journals and has a variety of contacts with the scientific community, and assesses as a matter of course the ideas emanating from these sources. Communication within the firm is well organized and co-ordinated and there is a willingness to share knowledge with other firms. The progressive firm also tends to set its standards by reference to best practice elsewhere, and makes provision for extensive overseas travel. We should also repeat here the importance of an effective marketing policy and good technical service to customers. When a firm undertakes a product innovation, one of the major determinants of its success is how quickly users adopt the new product. Obviously at this stage the co-ordination of production and marketing activities is all important.

So much, then, for the characteristics of the innovators. The rate of diffusion will also be a function of the various characteristics of the innovation itself. We deal with this in two parts: first, we consider in turn the main features of innovations that appear to affect the diffusion rate; secondly, we briefly survey some empirical tests of models of the diffusion process.

The most obvious point to make is that the speed of diffusion will be faster, the greater is the improvement over existing methods or goods represented by the new process or product. This can be seen clearly from Figure 7.2. For any given age distribution of the industry's existing capital stock, the greater the operating cost advantage of the new process, the more existing plants will it be worth while to scrap. Thus, ignoring difficulties of obtaining new process plant, the more rapidly will the new process spread. It must be emphasized that the important point is not only the cost advantage of the new process, but whether firms are aware of these advantages. This indicates the importance of communication and of firms' ability to assess the merit of technological advances.[2] Thus, even if a firm does not have a large scale research and development department, some research and development and employment of technically qualified personnel is necessary to screen new techniques, or to see

---

[1] C. Carter and B. Williams, op. cit., p. 177.
[2] The analysis, as we have indicated, can also be applied to product innovations in industry.

the possibilities of adopting new techniques to the firm's needs. Awareness of the advantages also implies the use of rational invest- ment appraisal. The wrong appraisal method can mean that old machines are not replaced as rapidly as it is profitable to do so. In a study of firms' replacement decisions, Nield found that in the U.K. two-thirds of engineering firms used a simple pay-off period criterion and, of these, 80% used a period of five years or less.[1] This represents a friction in the adjustment process.

The age structure of an industry's capital stock will influence the speed with which new processes are adopted. Let us take the follow- ing examples and assume in each case that the industry has only three vintages of machines, and that in each case the new process has the same operating cost advantage over techniques of the most recent vintage.

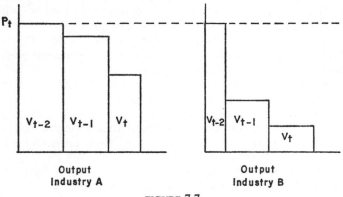

FIGURE 7.7

Industry B, in Figure 7.7, has a large number of plants of recent vintage, whereas industry A is currently producing a relatively larger proportion of its output with machines of older vintages. Diffusion, at least initially, will occur much more rapidly in the latter case, where many old plants will be worth scrapping. The existence of many recent plants has undoubtedly impeded the diffusion of the oxygen steel process. Oxygen steel plant is cheaper both in terms of capital cost and operating cost, than open-hearth steel plant. The first oxygen steel plant was introduced in Austria, in 1952. In the late 1940s and the early 1950s, even after the introduction of oxygen steel, large amounts of open-hearth capacity had been installed in France, Germany, Italy, and the U.K. The significant operating cost ad- vantage of oxygen steel plants has not been enough to make it worth

[1] R. Nield, 'Replacement Policy', *National Institute Economic Review*, 1964.

while to scrap many of the later open-hearth plants. In 1967, the proportion of total steel output produced by the oxygen process was 17% in France, 32% in Germany, 27% in Italy, and 28% in the U.K.[1] Although other influences have been at work, the age-structure of the industry's plant in the 1950s has undoubtedly been a major factor in the slow rate of diffusion of this process.

There is one important way in which a relatively high proportion of old equipment is an obstacle to diffusion. This is where the introduction of a new process depends upon the existence of up to date complementary equipment. An example of this can be found in railways. Improvements, such as electrification, which increase train speeds can normally be introduced only where the track is fully modernized and where automatic signalling equipment which incorporates automatic train control mechanisms is in use.

A third influence is the size of the capital outlay necessary to adopt the innovation. We have seen that the firm, faced with the decision to replace a machine, compares the operating cost of the old machine with the operating cost of the new machine, *plus* the amount necessary to yield a normal profit on its capital investment. The greater is the necessary investment (basically the purchase price of the new machine), the greater has the difference in operating costs to be. To put it another way: for any difference in operating costs, the smaller the purchase price of the machine, the more rapidly will replacement—and hence diffusion—occur.

The purchase price also affects the diffusion process because of risk. Innovation—especially for early adopters—involves risk, and it is probably true to say that risks will be more easily accepted where the sums of money involved are small, than where they are large. More generally, the greater the risk attached to an innovation, the more slowly will it spread. Willingness to accept risks varies between firms and between industries, and in rapidly growing firms or industries, and in those which are very secure financially, innovations will tend to spread relatively rapidly. This factor introduces two other important characteristics of an innovation. First, innovations that are 'divisible', in the sense that they may be experimented with on a small scale, will tend to diffuse relatively quickly—as innovation will imply no large scale commitment of resources at any one time. Secondly, in some cases, the initial uncertainty associated with a new process or product is reduced quite rapidly. Thus, reduced uncertainty among potential users speeds the diffusion process. The rate of reduction of uncertainty over time will also play a part in determining the speed with which a new technique is adopted *within* firms. The diesel locomotive and the use of special processes in paper-making,

[1] G. Ray, *op. cit.*, pp. 41–6.

are two examples of innovations where adoption was possible initially on a small scale, while older techniques were responsible for the major proportion of output. Where operation of complete plants has to be changed, which is usually the case in the heavy chemical industry, this method of reducing uncertainty cannot be used.

The factors we have been discussing are, in general, the most important influences on the rate of diffusion among firms. Certainly, models which have included these five variables have 'explained' diffusion processes. It is clear, however, that there are a multitude of influences which would retard or speed up the diffusion process. The range of influences on diffusion rates widens further when we consider innovations whose potential users are consumers or farmers. In these latter cases sociological forces will also play an important role. For example, the rate of adoption will be faster, the more compatible an innovation is with the existing values and past experiences of the adopters. An obvious example is the resistance to birth control in underdeveloped countries. Rogers cites the case of Australian farmers who have been observed to adopt mechanical innovations—which are compatible with their values—faster than non-mechanical innovations. He also emphasizes that it is compatibility, as perceived, that is the important factor. In the U.S.A., for example, 24% of upper class families in a survey had adopted television, by 1956, whereas 72% of working class families were adopters. Canasta (a card-game) has been adopted by 72% of the upper class families, but by only 12% of working class families.

Voluntary staying-on at school can be seen as an innovation. Sociological forces are important here, too. Trends in voluntary enrolment ratios seem to follow the same sort of growth path that we have described, but it is clear that for forecasting purposes one ideally needs to know the enrolment ratios for each social class separately.[1]

There are also some product innovations which seem to spread rapidly, simply because the user is hopelessly 'out of it' if he does not have the product. Television sets are an example.

Consumers and farmers will be influenced by the same sort of factors as those we have discussed with respect to firms. The adoption rate will be relatively rapid for those innovations which are divisible in the sense that they may be experimented with on a small scale. Early adopters may place the greatest emphasis on divisibility. Innovations whose results are easy to communicate to others will tend to be diffused relatively rapidly, e.g. pre-emergent weed-killers were slow to diffuse because there were no dead weeds for farmers to observe. The complexity of an innovation will also determine how

[1] See J. Vaizey, K. Norris and J. Sheehan, *The Political Economy of Education*. London, Duckworth, 1972, ch. 6.

fast it is adopted. In farm innovations this is the most important factor of all.

As in the case of firms, we might expect new products which absorb a negligible proportion of consumer income to diffuse relatively rapidly. We do not know of any systematic test of this hypothesis, but it is possible to think of counter examples. Motor-cars, for instance, which are expensive, have diffused fairly rapidly, whereas consumers were slow to adopt the safety razor.

Random influences will affect the rate of diffusion. We have seen, for example, how the Second World War retarded the spread of motor-cars and mono television in this country. Innovation in education was retarded during the War and in the Depression. In education, the diffusion process is heavily influenced by the presence of committed individuals. Innovations, such as educational television, which are expensive in absolute terms, require a champion who can successfully obtain finance. Some educational innovations, such as the use of specially prepared learning material, require dedicated teachers who are willing to sacrifice leisure time. These innovations tend to diffuse slowly.[1] In some cases a crisis reveals the merits of an innovation. The proportion of Wisconsin farmers adopting grass silage rose from 16% in 1950 to 48% in 1951. This sudden jump was largely due to rain and cold weather, in 1951, which made the cutting of hay difficult.

We now briefly summarize some attempts to explain formally the rate of diffusion of certain innovations. Mansfield tested four propositions on data regarding the diffusion of fourteen innovations in the U.S.A.[2] The four propositions are that: (i) the length of time a firm waits before adopting a new technique is inversely related to its size, (ii) as the size of a firm increases, the length of time it waits tends to decrease at an increasing rate; (iii) the delay is inversely related to the expected profitability of the innovation; and (iv) the delay reduces at an increasing rate with profitability. All of these propositions appear to be validated by the empirical evidence. One interesting result is that the 'elasticity of delay with respect to firm size' seems to be about -0.4. The results are also consistent with the hypothesis that the speed of diffusion is negatively related to the size of the initial investment required. One very interesting and rather surprising result that Mansfield obtained was that, if a firm is among the first to adopt a certain innovation, the chances of it being quick to adopt the subsequent innovation are not much better than evens.

[1] See J. Vaizey, E. Hewton and K. Norris, *The Costs of New Educational Technologies*, Lisbon, Gulbenkian Foundation, 1971.
[2] E. Mansfield, 'The Speed of Response of Firms to New Technologies', *Quarterly Journal of Economics*, 1963.

The fact that large firms were quicker to adopt innovations than small firms appears to some extent to be arithmetically inevitable. If we have an industry with two firms, one with 90% of the market, and the other with 10%, the large firm, if it innovates at an 'average' rate, will be first nine times out of ten. So, unless large firms introduce less than their share of innovations, they will tend to adopt faster than small firms. Metcalfe found that diffusion rates increase with size of firm in the Lancashire textile industry.[1] The study of diffusion of technologies in Western Europe that we have referred to on several occasions has produced rather mixed evidence on this hypothesis. Although, in the majority of cases, large firms were among the first to adopt new techniques, this was not true in the diffusion of oxygen steel. In some innovations large firms were among the leaders in some countries but not in others.

Finally, we refer again to Griliches's pioneer study of the diffusion of hybrid corn. Figure 7.4 showed that there were significant differences between states in the date at which the innovation was first adopted and in the speed at which the innovation was diffused. Griliches showed that for each state the value of the three parameters of the logistic growth curve could be explained by economic analysis. It will be remembered that the equation for the logistic growth curve, which is held to fit the diffusion process is:

$$P = \frac{K}{1 + \exp\{-(a + bt)\}}$$

The parameter a gives the date of origin, defined as the date when an area began to plant 10% of its ceiling average with hybrid corn, and thus fixes the curve on the horizontal axis. Griliches shows that these dates were largely determined by seed producers ranking areas according to profitability. They first entered the most profitable areas, in terms of the amount of corn acreage, likely equilibrium levels and marketing costs.

The coefficient b gives the rate of diffusion. Differences in the speed of adoption between states can be explained by differences in the profitability of hybrid seed relative to open, pollinated seed. These differences further determine K which gives the equilibrium proportion of corn acreage devoted to hybrid corn.

What is clear from the evidence is that the successful application of a new innovation implies much more than technical expertise. A whole host of complementary factors are important, and any individual firm is always liable to be retarded in its innovation by the slowness of others. On the supply side an absolute shortage of com-

[1] J. Metcalfe, *op. cit.*, p. 157.

ponents (products) may hinder adoption or, perhaps more important, suppliers may be slow or unwilling to adapt themselves to meet changing requirements. On the demand side, innovation may be impeded by a failure of customers to perceive the advantages of new products. Many new products are producer goods and it is thus apparent that a group of 'laggards' can have adverse effects on the rate of diffusion of innovation, both among their suppliers and among their customers. Rapid diffusion of an innovation is therefore facilitated where there is a willingness on the part of other people, as well as the particular firm in question, to make adjustments. This willingness is especially true of labour, but we leave the effect of technical advance on labour, and the role of labour in technical advance, to a later chapter.

Let us end this chapter by noting that the factors aiding and hindering diffusion which we have discussed in the context of the firm or the industry would appear to apply with at least equal force at a national level: 'What is suggested is that the needs for "embodiment" of a new technology transcend the creation of new physical capital. New investment in human capital in formal training and experience, and the investment of time and effort into remoulding or creating new institutions, are required as well.'[1] We will look again at this contention in Chapter 11.

[1] R. Nelson, M. Peck and E. Kalachek, *op. cit.*, p. 108.

CHAPTER 8

The Public Sector

In the U.K., as in most industrialized countries, the government plays a dominant role in scientific and technological activities. The government finances about half of all expenditure on research and development, employs about half of all qualified scientists and engineers, and is responsible for the higher education of almost all skilled manpower. Government influence is not spread equally over the various activities we have examined and is particularly strong in science and basic research.

TABLE 8.1. *Percentage of Research and Development Financed by Government, 1967*

Austria	40
Belgium	23
Canada	55
Denmark	59
France	48
West Germany	46
Ireland	52
Italy	17
Japan	30
The Netherlands	40
Norway	61
Spain	65
Sweden	42
U.K.	51
U.S.A.	64

Source: UNESCO Statistical Yearbook, 1969, Paris, 1970.

The figures in Table 8.1 show that the proportion of research and development supported by the government in the U.K. is neither particularly high nor low, at least as far as developed countries are concerned.

The precise ways in which this expenditure is distributed varies between countries. In countries with high defence expenditures or with large aerospace industries, a disproportionate share of government expenditure is claimed by these two sectors. This is the case, as we shall see, in the U.K.; and from now on we shall confine our attention to the U.K. First, we examine the allocation of government expenditure on research and development and briefly describe the main agencies responsible for the expenditure.

ALLOCATION OF GOVERNMENT EXPENDITURE

The first point to emphasize is that the proportion of research and development *undertaken* by the government is much less than the proportion it finances. In 1967, the government sector undertook 24·8% of all research and development. An analysis of the total U.K. research effort by sources of finance and by location of the activity is given in Table 8.2.[1]

It can be seen from the first column of the table that the amount of research and development undertaken by the government sector, but which is non-government financed, is very small. Thus, in our discussion of the government effort we shall concentrate on that financed by the government as shown in the first row of Table 8.2. The expenditure can be divided according to the sector undertaking the work, as in the table. There are five major sectors and we consider each in turn.

We start with government intra-mural research, which accounts for about 44% of the total. Table 8.3 gives a breakdown of this research: it is only possible to do this for current expenditure. Not all of the data represent *scientific* research and development.

The most striking feature of all this work is the dominance of defence. Although there may be some spillover effects into the civil sector this research and development is obviously undertaken largely for motives unconnected with the advance of civil scientific and technological knowledge. The atomic-energy sector claims a significant proportion of intra-mural expenditure, and a high proportion of this expenditure is devoted to development work. This is also true of defence.

In the civil sector, expenditure is relatively evenly spread between basic research, applied research and development. The research expenditure is largely concentrated in the Research Councils, which are autonomous bodies, incorporated by Royal Charter and receiving virtually all of their income from the central government (i.e. Department of Education and Science). There are five Research Councils: the Agricultural Research Council, founded in 1931; the Medical

[1] Some figures are available for later years. For comparative purposes, however, we use the latest year for which we have comprehensive statistics.

TABLE 8.2. *Research and Development Expenditure: U.K., 1967*

Sector providing the funds	Sector Carrying out the Work						Total Amount Financed by each Sector (£ thousand)
	Government	Universities and Further Education Establishments*	Public Corporations	Research Associations	Private Industry	Other	
Government†	217,265	61,517‡	433	4,486	196,012	13,391	493,104‡
Universities	—	5,700	—	—	—	—	5,700
Public corporations	§	400	39,212	1,046	3,559	266	44,483
Research associations	§	—	—	286	370	57	713
Private industry	8,862	3,000	1,443	5,970	335,708¶	5,048	360,031
Overseas	5,423	1,400	534	1,172	21,585	160	30,274
Other	7,124	3,147	10	—	12,603	4,878	27,762
Total cost of research and development carried out in each sector	238,674	75,174	41,632	12,960	569,837	23,800	962,067

Source: Department of Education and Science, *Statistics of Science and Technology*, London, HMSO, 1970.

* Academic year, 1966–67.
† The figures in this line are based on returns from the sectors carrying out the work.
‡ Including £1,849,000 financed by local government.
§ Included in private industry.
¶ Research and development budgets. Other monies earned (about £12·6 million) by R & D departments of private industry and used for their R & D programmes are included under 'Other'.

106

TABLE 8.3. *Government Current Expenditure on Intra-mural Research and Development, 1967*

	Percentage of Total Current Intra-mural Expenditure	Percentage of (1) that is:		
		Basic Research	Applied Research	Development
	(1)	(2)	(3)	(4)
Defence	49·9*	6·2	21·9	71·9
Technology (industrial services, aerospace and atomic energy)	27·1	13·7	22·7	63·6
Roads and transport	1·2	—	100·0	—
Research councils	13·8	68·7	30·7	0·6
Agriculture, forestry and fisheries	2·2	13·3	65·3	21·4
Financial administration	2·7	2·2	95·6	2·2
Other	3·1	1·6	65·0	33·4
Total Civil	50·1	27·1	35·3	37·6
Total	100*	18·9	28·0	53·1

Source: Department of Education and Science, *op. cit.*
* Includes some expenditure not allocated to the three categories.

Research Council (1913); the Natural Environmental Research Council (1965); the Science Research Council (1965); and the Social Science Research Council (1965). The purpose of the Research Councils is to foster research in their area of interest, and this they do by undertaking research themselves, and by financing post-graduate training, and research in universities, research associations and in independent institutes.

Only part of the expenditure of the Research Councils is devoted to research undertaken by themselves, the rest being used to support research in the universities and research associations; and hence only part is relevant to an analysis of government intramural research. Changes to the Research Council system were proposed in 1972—we shall discuss these later in this chapter together with the whole question of the allocation of resources to science.

About £60 million is spent by the government in support of research at universities and other further education establishments in the education sector. The education sector does little or no development work, devoting its resources in more or less equal proportions to basic and applied research. (See Table 8.4.)

TABLE 8.4. *Current Research and Development Expenditure Within the Education Sector, 1967* (£m.)

Basic research	31·7
Applied research	31·3
Development	0·2
	63·2

Source: Department of Education and Science, *op. cit.*

Funds from the government sector largely reach the universities in two ways: through the University Grants Committee, and through the Research Councils. The Research Councils' contribution amounted, in 1967, to about £19 million and took three forms—research grants, expenditure on research units located in or at universities and expenditure on research units associated with universities. The rest of the funds for university research came from the University Grants Committee, largely in the form of general grants rather than funds earmarked for specific purposes. Staff at universities also undertake a small amount of research for private industry.[1]

These expenditure figures understate the importance of education

---

[1] For an analysis of the ways in which co-operation between the universities and industry might be improved, see *Industry, Science, and Universities*, London, CBI, 1970.

in scientific and technological activities. Expenditures on the teaching of science and technology are excluded; yet it is through imparting knowledge and skills that education makes its greatest contribution to the advance of scientific and technological knowledge. Shortage of space prevents much discussion of this role: to be worth while such a discussion would have to be extensive.[1]

A small amount of government-financed research and development is carried out by Research Associations. These date from 1918, and there are fifty such associations. They are financed jointly by private industry and by the government, with government support being given in some proportion to the funds raised from industry. Research associations are essentially organizations which undertake research of collective interest to their members. They are organized on an industrial basis and about two-thirds of the manufacturing, construction and utilities industries are served by associations. As co-operative ventures they are most important in industries which are not research intensive and where the typical unit is small.[2] Associations are not suited to industries where one or two firms have a dominant position. Research associations with a high industrial coverage include cotton, cutlery, furniture, lace and wool. The formation of research associations is the natural response to a situation where firms are unable or unwilling to establish a research and development department of their own, and to situations where innovation is not a powerful form of competition. The work of the research associations reflects this, and is more concerned with unspectacular improvements and modifications than with significant technological advance. Research associations do undertake some basic research, however, although it is largely mission orientated. As a group, basic research accounts for about a quarter of their activities, development for about a half, and the rest of their work is in providing information services for members.[3] In carrying out this latter function, associations in effect screen relevant research and development results for their members, and the results of work done by associations is made available to all members. Patent income accrues to the association, but members normally obtain licences on a preferential basis.

Research associations, then, play a small but significant role in industrial research, where the conditions are favourable to co-operative research and development. The role of the government is to put up about half of their finance and, through its representatives on

[1] The interested reader may care to refer to J. Vaizey, K. Norris and J. Sheehan, *op. cit.*, especially Chs 1, 2, 7, 8, 9, 10.
[2] The vehicle industry is an exception to the latter proposition.
[3] *Industrial Research Associations in the United Kingdom*, Paris, OECD, 1967.

boards, the government scientific service may exert some influence on the direction of the work of the associations.

In 1967, the government spent £196 million on research and development carried out by private industry. This was not only a significant proportion (40%) of all government expenditure on research and development, but it represented one-third of all research and development undertaken in private industry. Government support for industrial research and development is heavily biased towards a few industries—with one industry, aerospace, claiming two-thirds of the total. The shares of the large industrial recipients of government finance are shown in Table 8.5. It is clear that we are entitled to ignore the government as a significant source of finance in industries, other than electronics, telecommunications and aerospace.

TABLE 8.5. *Allocation of Government Research-and-Development Expenditure in Private Industry, 1967/8*

	(£m.)	Percentage of Total
Electronics (including com-Puters) and telecommunications	47·9	24·4
Aerospace	131·0	66·8
All other private industry	17·1	8·8
	196·0	100·0

Source: Department of Education and Science, *op. cit.*

The aircraft industry is an interesting example of the spin-off in civil life of development work undertaken almost entirely for military purposes. The first aircraft—extremely cheaply built by amateurs and small garages in the period just before the First World War—were soon taken up by the armed forces of France, Germany, the U.S.A. and the U.K., and development work proceeded with the help of the armed forces and financial support from governments. During the First World War, aircraft were used for bombing and spotting, and as fighters. Early civil aviation immediately after the First World War was based largely upon converted bombers, and the developments in civil aviation between the Wars were largely based on the successive improvements in these aircraft, which had been fundamentally designed for military purposes.

The technical developments which occurred were mainly in the realm of fighter aircraft, which were too small for civilian passenger-carrying purposes, and in the development of seaplanes, which were regarded as a major technical innovation that would enable the flexibility of aviation to be maximized.

110

Major steps took place during the Second World War, and included the development of radar and radio, the building of airfields, the creation of a heavy bomber force and of the jet engine; and it was on the basis of these airfields, technological equipment and the heavy bombers that civil aviation took a real step forward after the War. Since then, the greater part of the overhead expenses of the aerospace industry in all countries has been borne directly or indirectly on the defence budget. It can be shown that, but for this defence budget, there would not now be aircraft of the size, speed and technical sophistication which exist for civil aviation purposes, and that many of the world's major airports would not, in turn, exist.

The primary purpose of the development of aviation has been the attempt on the part of major powers to keep a step ahead of one another militarily. In the first place, this rivalry was largely between the U.K., France and Germany; subsequently it became a rivalry between the U.S.S.R. and the U.S.A., a rivalry which to all intents and purposes has now ceased in aviation but not in the aerospace field. It is for this reason that most of the major developments in civil aviation, like Concorde, have been revealed to be as expensive as they are because they are no longer by-products of a hidden, defence budgetary cost.

The determination of total expenditures on defence and aerospace is a very complex issue. Once the global level of expenditure is fixed, the related expenditure on research and development is essentially predetermined. Large scale technology projects, such as aerospace programmes, may influence the economy in three ways. There will be a direct impact on a network of supplier firms. Secondly, a transfer of technology may occur from the project to other fields, which will be effected largely through supplier firms. Thirdly, there has been a tendency, observed especially in the U.S.A., for individuals involved in large scale projects to take advantage of their specialized knowledge by setting up their own firms. Science based firms of this sort have also been established by men who have left the research and development departments of large industrial corporations.

The second of these three effects, i.e. the technical benefits which accrue to firms other than the sponsor, has been termed 'spin-off', and it is often suggested that this is the main external benefit of aerospace and defence programmes. There is some evidence on the nature of these benefits from the Concorde project.[1] The Concorde project necessitated the solution of some novel technical problems, such as overcoming the adverse effects of high temperatures on the airframe and engines. The pay-load was a relatively small proportion

[1] *Aspects of Spin-Off*, London, Centre for the Study of Industrial Innovation, 1971.

of total weight, which led to an emphasis on the development of low weight materials, and the control and navigation systems also had to operate to a more stringent requirement, because of higher speeds. Thus, although Concorde did not represent a technological breakthrough, since the development of military aircraft had overcome the major difficulties associated with supersonic flight, the combination of supersonic speeds and civil aviation requirements did pose technical problems.

About six-hundred U.K. supplier firms were associated with the manufacture of the prototypes and the two pre-production aircraft. About one-third of the sample reported that the technical specifications that had to be met by components supplied to Concorde were more stringent than those usually demanded. This immediately limited spin-off to only one-third of suppliers. The stringency of specifications led to some 'stretching' of research and development departments and involved the handling of new materials, adoption of new techniques, and generally involved 'the sharpening of existing technological capabilities to achieve new performance criteria rather than a completely new breakthrough in technology'. The effects on production were similar and, in 14% of companies supplying materials to the Concorde project, meant the adoption of processes that were new to the firms. More general spin-off benefits included the possibility of firms using materials that were developed for Concorde in non-Concorde work, and a generally increased technological capability. Some spin-off benefits included in the Report, such as the advantages to a company of being able to use its participation in the project as part of an advertising campaign seem to represent pecuniary rather than technological spill-over effects.

Defence and aerospace programmes that involve fundamental technological advances are likely to have greater spill-over effects. Defence orientated research and development was, for example, at least partly responsible for the computer and for atomic energy. Such effects are best treated as incidental benefits from expenditure which has other objectives and should not be used as a justification for such expenditure. No one has yet, in any case, succeeded in quantifying these spin-off effects. They certainly exist, but could almost certainly be obtained more cheaply in other ways.

Another form of a governmental link with the private sector is the role played by the National Research Development Corporation. This organization was established in 1949 and has two broad objectives. First, it aims to secure the exploitation and development of inventions resulting from public sector research or of any other invention which it appears is not being 'adequately exploited'. This function is by far the more important. Public sector research results are usually exploited by licensing arrangements, both in the U.K. and abroad. The Corporation is expected to be financially self-supporting and over half of its income comes from licensing arrangements. The Corporation also supports development projects being undertaken by firms. The second objective of the Corporation is to promote and assist research aimed at specific practical requirements.

The National Research Development Corporation necessarily attracts long term, high risk projects whose burden private industry is unwilling or unable to assume. It also tends to support projects whose social returns are likely to be in excess of their private returns, and to the extent that it chooses wisely it can correct a possible misallocation of resources.

So far we have discussed the research and development work that is financed by the government and carried out, either by the government itself, or by universities, research associations and private industry. This leaves a residual expenditure of about £14 million (see Table 8.2), which includes the research and development expenditures of the public corporations and also payments to individuals and to private research organizations.

This completes our survey of the allocation of government expenditures. If we leave aside expenditures on defence, electronics and aerospace, it is apparent that the public sector's activities are relatively biased towards research. In 1967, in fact, 75% of all basic research was located in the public sector. For this reason, it is convenient to consider the rationale of basic research in the present chapter, but much of the argument applies to basic research undertaken in the private sector.

SCIENTIFIC RESEARCH

The results of pure scientific research are not patentable and, hence, in general the sponsor of such research is not able to appropriate the returns. The returns to basic research will tend, as we shall see, to be widely diffused and returns in the form of innovations may occur decades or even generations after the research was finalized. There is therefore a strong presumption that the social returns to expenditure on research will exceed the private returns. The result is that, in the absence of government support, the economy may tend to under-invest in basic research. Hirschleifer has challenged the conventional view that patent protection is necessary to avoid under-investment in inventive activity on the ground that the inventor will be able to take advantage of increases in asset values that follow an invention (see Chapter 3). This argument cannot be applied to basic research—for this will rarely have any immediate or clearly foreseeable economic impact—nor, in general, to applied research.

A major role of the government in research and development is to correct this potential misallocation by subsidies, or by directly undertaking or sponsoring research in the public sector. The argument that some basic research should be carried out by the public sector does not, unfortunately, enable us to decide how many resources society should devote to science. As economists, faced with such a question as this, we can always set up one of our neat principles, such as that scientific activities should be pursued until the (discounted) net social marginal returns are zero. This does not get us very far in practice, as we can rarely measure the benefits or losses which arise from science, although, as we shall see, it has proved possible to do this in one or two specific cases. The most fundamental difficulty is probably that scientific activities are pursued for a number of reasons and with a number of objectives in mind. In so far as these objectives are fulfilled science will have multiple outputs.

The benefits arising from scientific research can be divided into four broad groups: direct benefits of mission orientated research; benefits of the economic application of curiosity orientated research; manpower benefits; and cultural benefits. We consider each of these benefits in turn and look at attempts to measure them.

The term 'mission orientated research' is applied to research that is undertaken with specific objectives, or research whose ultimate application is evident. The objectives of mission orientated research need not necessarily be commercial objectives and, to that extent, the term is not precisely synonymous with 'applied research'. Research with clear objectives is commonly undertaken in agriculture and medicine, and there are published studies of the returns to specific research projects in these areas.

One of the earliest empirical studies of this sort was carried out by Griliches,[1] who estimated the social rate of return to investment in hybrid corn research. The costs incurred by society can be divided into research costs and the cost of additional resources devoted to the production of hybrid seed. Both public and private expenditures on research were taken into account. It was assumed that an annual expenditure of some $3 million will continue, in perpetuity; no returns are imputed to it. There are other costs to be included, notably the additional cost of hybrid seed over seed that would otherwise be used. The difference is estimated at $9.50 per bushel in 1955, and it is possible from figures of acreages planted with hybrid corn over the relevant period (1911–55) to calculate the total costs in 1955 prices. The benefits from research in hybrid corn were that corn yields are higher from hybrid corn. A conservative

[1] Z. Griliches, 'Research Costs and Social Returns: Hybrid Corn and Related Innovations', *Journal of Political Economy*, 1958.

estimate is that yields are 15% above those from alternative seed. Now, the extra yields are valued by the loss in corn production that would have resulted from there being no hybrid corn.

In Figure 8.1, assume current price is OP_1, with amount OQ_1 consumed. The effect of there being no hybrid corn is shown by a vertical shift in the supply curve. The loss to society is given by the area $P_1 P_2$ AC which comprises the extra cost of producing the reduced level of corn output $P_1 P_2$ AB, plus the loss of consumers surplus ABC. This area is approximately measured by $k P_1 Q_1$ $(1 - \frac{1}{2} kn)$, where n is the elasticity of the demand curve, and k is the percentage change in yield. This is the basis of the calculation of benefits. Adjustment had to be made for the percentage of acreage devoted to hybrid corn, and for the tendency of the 1955 price of

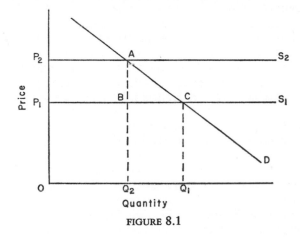

FIGURE 8.1

corn to overstate the social value of corn. The price is distorted by price support programmes. On these and other assumptions the internal rate of return to research expenditures is put at between 35% and 40%.[1]

Griliches suggests that this estimate is probably too low, since, whenever there were alternative assumptions, he made the ones which would minimize the rate of return. The rate of return as calculated is on applied research rather than on basic research. The basic research took place between 1905 and 1920 with minimal expenditure, and obviously the return to basic research would be higher. On the other hand, it is doubtful whether any such rate would have much meaning,

[1] The internal rate of return is the rate of discount which equates the flow discounted) costs and (discounted) benefits.

115

THE ECONOMICS OF RESEARCH AND TECHNOLOGY

since without the applied research many of the returns would pre-sumably not have materialized.

The rate of return as calculated is of course an *ex post* return on a successful invention—an invention, moreover, which is cited as one of the technological successes of the twentieth century. A result of the hybrid corn study that is of importance is that very few of the benefits were captured by the inventors or by the innovators. The benefits were widely spread and accrued in general to consumers in the form of lower prices and higher output. As this invention was not suitable for patenting, it follows that the private returns were less than the social returns with a possibility of under-investment in research and in seed production.

Another case, this time in medicine, where it has proved possible to relate economic effects to research, is the research which led to the development of anti-poliomyelitis vaccines. Weisbrod has attempted to measure the social rate of return to this research.[1] The benefits of poliomyelitis research that were quantified fall into three groups. First, reductions in mortality. Philosophical questions about the value of a life are avoided by taking into account only the market value of the net loss of production avoided by preventing death. Thus, the benefits are massively understated. When a person who is in the labour market (or potentially in the labour market) dies, then there is a loss of output which is measured by the discounted present value of his assumed future earnings. The loss to society is this amount less the discounted present value of his future consumption outlays. These amounts will vary according to the age and sex of those whose death is prevented. The second set of benefits are those that arise from reductions in morbidity, i.e. those resulting from the temporary loss of a producer. Reductions in morbidity are valued by the loss of production, whereas reductions in mortality are valued by reductions in production *less* reductions in consumption. With high marginal propensities to consume, this method places a higher value than one suspects that society would put on reductions in sickness relative to the value placed on saving life. Thirdly, society saves the resources previously devoted to the care of poliomyelitis victims.

Thus, it is apparent that a flow of social returns to polio research can be derived. The costs to be set against these benefits are the resources devoted to poliomyelitis research and to costs of vaccina-tions. Apart from data problems, there are difficulties in identifying which pieces of research have been devoted to the case of polio-myelitis. Research aimed at preventing other diseases may generate information on poliomyelitis and vice versa. Weisbrod derives,

[1] B. Weisbrod, 'Costs and Benefits of Medical Research: a Case Study of Poliomyelitis', *Journal of Political Economy*, 1971.

however, an estimate of the appropriate research expenditures. The costs of vaccination include the cost of the vaccine, the resources devoted to applying the vaccine and the time (production) lost when people have to travel to a hospital to be vaccinated. From the flow of social costs and returns a multitude of rates of return are calculated, based on various assumptions and time horizons. The 'most likely' rate of return seems to be 11–12%. The results are fairly sensitive to the assumptions made, and when some 'pessimistic' assumptions are combined the estimated return is negative. Although it has to be emphasized that the 'non-monetary benefits of preventing death' are specifically excluded, the rates of return seem surprisingly low. The return that would be captured by the inventor would probably be below the social return (for reasons already discussed), but in this case there is a further reason for supposing that a market solution might not be optimal. This is that polio is a contagious disease and a consumer when deciding whether to purchase vaccine takes into account only the benefits accruing to him and ignores the decreased risk of others contracting polio that would result from his purchase. Too little vaccine would be demanded, which—in the market solution—would reduce the return to research.

It is obvious that, because of the multitude of assumptions and guesses that have to be made in calculating the return to a successful piece of basic research, the estimates can only hope to indicate the rough order of magnitude of the returns, and no great accuracy is claimed for the results.

It is not clear what conclusions are to be drawn from these results, ignoring their probably wide error margins. Basic research is a risky undertaking, and therefore it is to be expected that the *ex post* return should be high (not that the return to polio research is high when compared with the returns to investment in fixed assets). The analogy often drawn is with the return on a successful oil well. The *ex post* return is very high, while the *ex ante* return, which reflects the probability of success, is very much lower. The results from specific studies cannot be generalized. Hybrid corn and polio research were presumably chosen for study precisely because these were research projects whose costs and benefits could be estimated with some accuracy. Even with mission orientated research this has not often proved to be possible. Studies of this sort are useful, for even if the estimated rates of returns are subject to error such work does indicate the ways in which benefits are diffused and to whom they accrue. The fact remains, however, that we have only a handful of estimates of the social benefits of applied research and it is clear that the allocation of resources to research has in general to be decided in some other way.

117

Now let us consider the second of the four groups of benefit that arise from scientific research. Here we are concerned with the economic benefits of curiosity orientated research. The most obvious way in which basic research can have positive effects on output is when advances in science lead to changes in technology. The effect is multiplied as most technological change simply builds upon previous technology. The time-lag between scientific advance and any subsequent change in technology may be very long and has typically been rather less than a generation. For example, Faraday's work on electromagnetic generation, around 1830, was the scientific base of the heavy electrical engineering industry, some fifty years later. The basic science responsible for semiconductors was undertaken about eighteen years before the industrial application. There is little agreement among scientists as to whether this time-lag is lengthening or shortening. Apart from direct causal effects such as this, the myriad results of basic research may tend to lead to a host of minor changes in industrial methods and products. In these cases, the benefits of science will be widely spread. Another advantage that is of some importance is the listening post function of basic research. Personnel actively involved in scientific activity are those most able to screen research results and to identify possible industrial applications.

A method of quantifying these benefits of basic research has been suggested.[1] The starting point is the notion that basic research may lead to new industries, or may have smaller scale applications in industry. The method is, then, to see (using discounted cash flow techniques) what effect a notional delay in the scientific discovery would have had on the net benefits from the discovery. The net benefits are measured by the change in output *less* the costs of applied research, development, investment and manufacturing. This was a very ambitious procedure, and the Council for Scientific Policy sponsored a study into the feasibility of applying this method. This work showed that, although in some cases it is possible to trace the economic benefits of a scientific discovery, the Byatt–Cohen method is in general not feasible. The reason is that the interaction between science and technology is too complex to be amenable to the sort of analysis suggested. Thus, it is rarely possible to relate an innovation to a piece of basic research. We have referred earlier to the analysis of innovations which won the Queen's Award to Industry.[2] Eighty-four innovations were studied, and in only two cases was it possible to identify an associated scientific discovery. Even where it is possible

---

[1] I. Byatt and A. Cohen, *An Attempt to Quantify the Economic Benefits of Scientific Research* (*Science Policy Studies No. 4*), London, HMSO, 1969.
[2] J. Langrish *et al.*, *op. cit.*

to identify an innovation with some basic research, the substantial time-lags mean that many other factors are operating to obscure the effect of notional delays. In some cases, it has been argued that a marginal delay in scientific discovery would have *added* to the benefit. For example, the Joule–Thompson effect was discovered in 1852, but the process was not used until 1895, when there was a large scale industrial demand for oxygen. It is suggested that, if the effect had been discovered later, industrial scientists would have been more familiar with it and exploited it earlier.

Thus, it has not proved possible to utilize the approach suggested by Byatt and Cohen. The principal reason for the method's failure is that the sequential causal process of basic science, applied science and innovation does not correspond to experience. Until the ways in which basic research becomes transferred into industrial innovation are known, there seems, at least to a non-scientist, to be little chance of measuring the economic benefits of basic research.

The remaining two groups of benefits can be more briefly examined. First, research plays a part in the training of scientific manpower. To some extent this rests on the assertion that the best teachers are those who undertake research, and is anyway inextricably bound up with the benefits of education. As there are severe difficulties in attempting to measure the returns to educating scientists, it does not seem possible to single out the contribution of scientific research. Finally, science has cultural benefits and society may derive pleasure from the national prestige that high quality scientific research may bring. It is not possible to measure such benefits—but their very existence adds to the problems of deciding the allocation of resources to science.

In conclusion, some advances have been made in quantifying some of the economic returns to scientific research. But it is, at present, not possible to measure many of the benefits. Scientific research is an activity with multiple objectives or outputs, and in such cases— education is another—there is rarely a consensus on the relative weights to be attached to each objective. Thus, even if it proves possible to quantify some outputs, no unambiguous resource allocation rules will emerge. However, studies that help us to understand more clearly the nature of the benefits and the causal mechanisms involved can only help decision makers, because the allocation of funds to scientific research in the public sector has to be decided on some criterion.

Little can be said about which forms of scientific research to support. National goals will play a part, as they did in the decision to support atomic energy in the U.K. The opinion of scientists seems to be that the main criterion, at least for basic research, should be the intellectual quality and promise of the work and, perhaps more important, of the men who will carry out the research.[1]

In 1972, some of the Research Councils' autonomy in deciding which lines of research to support was removed. This change of policy started from the principle that applied research should be undertaken on a customer–contractor basis—i.e. the customer, who in this case is usually a government department, should specify his requirements which the contractor, in this case a Research Council, then attempts to meet. Previously, the Research Councils determined their own research programme. It was argued that this is wrong: 'However distinguished, intelligent and practical scientists may be, they cannot be so well qualified to decide what the needs of the nation are, and their priorities, as those responsible for ensuring that those needs are met.'[2] It is proposed to remove from the Research Councils that proportion of their annual funds which is devoted to applied research, and such funds are to be transferred to relevant government departments—the customers—to contract out as they decide. It seems clear that the scientific community is to lose some of its power to decide the direction of its work.

CONCLUSIONS

The public sector accounts for a large proportion of research and development expenditure. Much of this expenditure is devoted to scientific, rather than technological, activities and as such has not proved very amenable to economic analysis. The question of 'national science policy' is a very broad one and we have chosen to discuss only those parts of it in which economic influences may be of at least potential importance. Much of the public sector's development activities in defence, atomic energy and aerospace are not primarily to be judged on economic grounds. The public sector is largely responsible for the education of highly qualified manpower, and decisions in this field will have a powerful impact on research and development activities in the private sector.

[1] See the comments of top scientists in: A. Rueck, M. Goldsmith and J. Knight (eds), *Decision Making in National Science Policy*, London, Churchill, 1968.
[2] *A Framework for Government Research and Development*, London, HMSO, 1971.

CHAPTER 9

Some International Questions

In various parts of this book we have made reference to the scale of research and development activity in different industrial countries. We have looked at the industrial distribution of research activities and at the scale of the support that the government gives to science and technology in different countries. In this chapter we bring together three further international aspects of technological change.

We first examine whether there is any tendency for countries which devote a relatively high proportion of their GNP to research and development to experience relatively fast rates of growth. The answer is that they do not. One reason for this is that science and technology which is developed in one country gets transferred in a number of ways to other countries. Thus, a country may undertake little research of its own and take advantage of changes in scientific knowledge and in technology emanating from other countries. The international transfer of science and technology is discussed in the second section of this chapter. Finally, we take a closer look at one country, Japan, which has followed a policy of capitalizing on research and development done elsewhere and of having a relatively small indigenous research effort.

EXPENDITURE ON RESEARCH AND DEVELOPMENT
AND GROWTH RATES

We saw, in Chapter 2, that expenditure on research and development as a percentage of GNP differs considerably between industrial countries. In the OECD countries this proportion varied, in 1963, from 0·2% in Spain and Portugal to 3·6% in the U.S.A. The figures are presented again in column (1) of Table 9.1. We also saw in the earlier chapter that in some countries, e.g. the U.S.A., a significant proportion of total expenditure was not undertaken with economic objectives. This was particularly true of defence expenditure. If there is to be a relationship between growth rates and research and development it should be stronger when only economically motivated research and development is considered.

If high research and development expenditures do lead to rapid growth, the effect will only materialize after an unknown time-lag. In practice, we are saved troubling too much over this lag as the earliest year for which we have reliable figures for a sizable sample of countries is 1963. In Table 9.1, we compare research and development expenditure in 1963 with the growth of output over the period 1960–68. This seems to imply that we expect research activity to affect output in some previous period. But research expenditures as a *proportion* of national output seem to change only slowly, so we are probably entitled to assume that the proportion in, say, 1959, was not much different from that in 1963.

It will be seen from Table 9.1 that there is no tendency for countries

TABLE 9.1. *Research and Development Expenditure and the Growth of Output*

	(1) R & D Expenditure as a Percentage of GNP at Factor Cost (1963)	(2) Economically Motivated R & D as a Percentage of GNP at Factor Cost (1963)	(3) Average Annual Rate of Growth of GNP per Head at Factor Cost (1960–68)
Austria	0·3	0·2	3·8†
Belgium	1·1	0·9	3·6
Canada	1·2	0·6	3·5
France	1·9	0·8	4·4§
Germany	1·6*	1·0*	3·4‡
Greece	0·2*	0·1*	6·3†
Ireland	0·5	0·4	3·2
Italy	0·7	0·4	4·4§
Japan	1·5	1·1	9·2‡,§
The Netherlands	2·1*	1·5*	3·9‡,§
Norway	0·8	0·4	4·1‡
Portugal	0·2*	0·1*	4·9
Spain	0·2*	0·1*	6·5§
Sweden	1·6	0·8	3·9‡
Turkey	0·4*	n.a.*	3·4
U.K.	2·6*	1·3*	2·3
U.S.A.	3·6	1·0	3·7

Sources: See Table 2.2 *United Nations Statistical Yearbook, 1970*, New York, 1971.
* 1964.
† 1960–67.
‡ 1960–69.
§ At market prices.

with large research and development expenditures to experience relatively rapid growth rates. This result obtains, both when all research and development expenditure is used, and when only economically motivated research and development expenditure is considered. The country with the fastest growth rate, Japan, has not been a particularly large spender on research and development. Statistically, in fact, there is a weak negative association, i.e. the countries who have devoted an above-average share of their output to research and development have, if anything, experienced below-average rates of growth.[1]

It is often argued that research and development leads to innovation which leads to growth. It should be clear by now, that for a variety of reasons this is too simple a notion. We will briefly outline the more obvious reasons why there is no observable relationship between research and development expenditure and growth.

The most obvious point to make is that research and development expenditure is but one of the influences on economic growth, and to expect to discover a clear relationship with growth is to ignore the effect of all the other influences.

The expenditure that is grouped as 'research and development' covers a wide range of activities. Leaving aside the statistical problem that some items are classified as research and development that are more properly considered as production, there is the question of the allocation of expenditure between research and development. Research can be taken as roughly corresponding to science, and development as roughly corresponding to technology. The ways in which changes in science and technology affect output and the growth of output are not known with any degree of precision; neither, as we saw in Chapter 8, is the relationship known between scientific progress and changes in technology. It is thought, however, that a change in technology will have a more direct and immediate effect on output than will a scientific advance. Thus, if we observed two countries with the same overall ratio of research and development to output, but with a different mix of basic research, applied research and development, we would not expect (other things being equal) to observe that the two countries had similar rates of growth. The research and development mix does vary considerably from one country to another. The two largest spenders, the U.K. and the U.S.A., devote a smaller proportion (about 11%) of their effort to basic research than do the other countries, but, on the other hand, they devote a larger proportion of expenditure to development. The business sector generally undertakes less basic research as a propor-

[1] The correlation between columns (1) and (3) is -0.25, and between columns (2) and (3) is -0.14. Neither correlation is significant.

tion of total expenditure than does the public sector. In some countries, such as The Netherlands, Austria and Japan, however, over 10% of business research and development is basic research.

In addition, the rate of growth of output per man depends crucially on the rate at which innovations are diffused. It counts for little if a country, through a high expenditure on research and development, makes significant inventions which are only innovated on a small scale, or perhaps not at all. Thus, our attention is drawn again to the importance of being able to 'manage' technological advances. Where (because of failure to realize the potential of an invention or because of resistance to change on the part of potential customers) innovation does not follow on a large scale, the potential productivity gains will not be captured.

Another reason for our failure to relate national research and development expenditure to the growth of output per head is perhaps the most important of all. This is that there is a considerable international flow of research results, scientific know-how and inventions embodied in a variety of forms, notably scientific publications, scientific personnel, licences, and capital goods. Thus, one country may benefit from research expenditures made in another country. The international transfer of science and technology merits more lengthy discussion and is considered in the subsequent section.

THE INTERNATIONAL TRANSFER OF SCIENCE AND TECHNOLOGY

The results of scientific research tend to be widely disseminated at low cost. Therefore, except where scientific research is closely linked with strategic objectives, any one country can obtain the results of scientific research located throughout the world. It is estimated that roughly three-quarters of the world's supply of basic research comes from just two countries—the U.S.S.R., and the U.S.A. So other countries, then, can obtain the advantages of scientific research without themselves actually undertaking much research. We have emphasized that, for a firm to take the fullest advantage of published research results, it is necessary for it to have some research facilities. Similarly, a country must have scientists carrying out basic research if they are to fulfil a listening post function. The major method by which scientific knowledge is transferred is through published work, although face to face contacts between scientists are also considered important.

It has been argued that the U.K. should reduce the scale of its scientific research.[1] The argument is that research will be undertaken

[1] E.g. by M. Peck, 'Science and Technology', in: R. Caves (ed.), *Britain's Economic Prospects*, London, Allen & Unwin, 1968.

by the U.S.A. and the U.S.S.R. for competitive reasons and the results of this research become international free goods. Evidence is cited which shows that the location of basic research does not always determine the location of innovation. Thus, the U.K. should have a smaller research establishment, mainly devoted to screening the results of overseas research and carrying out applied research. As the relationship between scientific advance and change in technology, or innovation, is not known, it is difficult to support or disprove this argument as it stands. The weakness of the argument is that it pre-supposes that research is undertaken solely in order to bring about innovations. Scientific activity has many objectives, including the furthering of educational and cultural aims, and it is also undertaken for reasons of national prestige. Unfortunately, we do not know how well it achieves such aims or how we are to weight these objectives.

We now move on to consider the ways in which technology is transferred from one country to another. Probably, the most important mode of transfer is through international trade in goods. Particularly important in this context is the trade in capital goods produced by research intensive industries. These producer goods embody technological change and it is through the purchase of these goods that a country can capture some of the benefits of technological change that has occurred elsewhere. There is evidence that the transfer of technology through trade in capital goods has increased rapidly, especially between the Western European countries and between the U.S.A., Japan and Canada.[1]

It is not only capital goods that embody advanced technologies. The same is true of consumer durable goods. Trade in consumer durable goods can have far reaching effects on less developed countries—learning to operate a car or a television set can be very modernizing. However, the controls imposed by such obstacles as tariffs, exchange control regulations, quotas, and transport costs, mean that we have to consider other forms of technology transfer.

Technology is also transferred through licensing arrangements. Licensing agreements may be made between independent firms or between parent and subsidiary companies. It is therefore difficult to distinguish the role of licensing from that of direct investment. Licensing, as such, is not thought to be a very important form of technology transfer. In 1967, the U.K. paid out £58·8 million in technological royalties and received £62·7 million. This rough balance in overseas technological royalty transactions can be compared with that of France and Germany, who spend roughly three times as much as they receive, and with that of the U.S.A. whose

[1] K. Pavitt, 'The Multi-national Enterprise and the Transfer of Technology' in: J. Dunning (ed.), *The Multi-national Enterprise*, London, Allen & Unwin, 1971.

income from this source exceeds its expenditure by a factor of ten. Firms often see licensing as a second, or third, best way of penetrating foreign markets, as when the licensee is an independent firm the licensor loses control over product know-how and product marketing. Licensing, however, often permits a firm to sell in markets that would otherwise be difficult to penetrate. The activities of Beechams in the U.S.A. are an example of this approach. Generally, the research intensive industries account, as we would expect, for a high proportion of overseas royalty transactions.[1]

Direct investment is almost certainly the most important institutional arrangement by which technology is transferred. It has been estimated that, in 1970, the total of all direct investments was running at around $90,000 million. Companies in the U.S.A. have been dominant in making direct investments, although the rate of growth of outward investment has considerably slackened in the last five years. U.S. companies accounted, in 1965, for about 10% of gross domestic fixed capital formation in the U.K., and for about $4\frac{1}{2}\%$ of fixed investment in the EEC countries.[2] Technological know-how is 'transplanted' from the parent to the subsidiary, or from one arm of a multi-national enterprise to another. It is suggested that this is a particularly potent form of transfer, because these corporations are able to marshal the resources to exploit new technologies fully. There may be the added advantage that the managerial skills necessary for successful innovation may also be transferred. In this context, the role of companies which are dominated by U.S. interests is usually emphasized. Most countries have to incur costs in order to gain these advantages. Inward investment may weaken the competitive position of the host country. If multi-national companies have large research and development activities in a host country, they may claim scarce resources which would otherwise be employed by firms in the host country. Evidence on this is confusing.[3] A survey has shown that U.S. firms locate only 4% of their research and development expenditures abroad. Research and development is more easily centralized than production, as the costs of transferring the results of these activities is small. Yet U.S. firms in the U.K. seem to spend more on research and development than do their indigenous competitors. The extent to which this research and development would not otherwise be undertaken is not clear. Other

[1] Firms in chemicals and engineering accounted for two-thirds of the overseas royalty transactions of the U.K. in 1967.

[2] J. Dunning, 'Technology, United States, Investment, and European Economic Growth', in: C. Kindleberger (ed.), *The International Corporation*, London, MIT Press, 1970.

[3] J. Dunning, *op. cit.*, p. 162.

writers have emphasized the political costs of inward investment. Foreign companies in some sense control significant proportions of the investment and the output of some host countries. Direct investment is but one way of obtaining technology, and little work has been done on the relative costs and advantages of each method.

In some cases it is relatively easy simply to observe and imitate production methods used abroad. Mass production methods for cars and welded ship construction are examples of technologies that have been transferred by imitation.

Finally, we should mention the transfer of technological know-how through the mobility of personnel and through personal contacts between technologists in different countries. We have already seen that one of the characteristics of technically progressive firms is that they possess a wide range of contacts with firms and the scientific community in other countries.

Most countries must obtain significant proportions of their technology from abroad. Apart from the U.S.A. and the U.S.S.R., no country can at present hope to produce more than, say, 10% of the world's scientific and technological knowledge. In the study of innovations which have won Queen's Awards to Industry, referred to earlier, it was found that, of the 158 ideas used in 51 innovations, 53 came from overseas. Hence, the importance of technology transfer.

We have seen that there are various ways in which a country can import technology. To take the fullest advantage of foreign technology, whichever method is used, a country must be capable of absorbing an advanced technology. Successful innovation, and rapid diffusion of innovation implies much more than technological knowledge, as we saw in Chapters 6 and 7. It is for this reason that the less developed nations are not able to absorb foreign technology to anything like the same extent as are advanced economics. Moreover, the technology developed in the advanced countries is usually not suited to the needs of less developed nations.

RESEARCH AND DEVELOPMENT IN JAPAN

The post-war experience of Japan is most interesting in this context. The rate of growth of output has been high, averaging 9–10%, and it is widely accepted that this growth has been largely based upon successful innovation, although it has been accompanied by a shift from primary to secondary industries. Yet Japan has devoted a relatively low proportion—about 1·5%—of its GNP to research and development. Government support of research and development has been small compared with many industrial countries, yet the share of basic research has been high. In addition, Japan has imported much of its technology. In this section we briefly outline the policies that have been followed in Japan.

Post-war policy has been to develop the chemical, electronics and engineering industries, and in most cases the basic technologies have been imported. The technology transfer has largely been brought about through licensing agreements. Such agreements have been mainly with American firms. Royalty payments, in 1967, amounted to about $250 million. This policy of importing technology has been accompanied by several other measures which have greatly contributed to its success.

There has been severe limitation on the domestic operations of foreign companies and domestic industries have been given protection from foreign competition. Also the government, through the agencies of the Ministry of International Trade and Industry, and the Japanese Development Bank, has exerted a strong influence on the nature of the technology that has been imported. At the same time, there has been a heavy investment in education and in training which has added to the capability of the economy to absorb advanced technologies. It should be emphasized that, in 1945, the average level of skills was already in excess of that possessed by the population of most of the less developed countries today.

The indigenous research and development effort, although relatively low in proportion to the GNP has been closely linked to imported methods. Between 1950 and 1963, for example, 1,500 companies received imported technology and, of these, 83% were undertaking related research and development. A high proportion, about 75%, of Japan's research and development effort is economically motivated and the share undertaken by the government is correspondingly low, about 30%. Thus, most of the indigenous research and development was part of an innovation process having imported technology as its core.

This policy has been operated so successfully that Japan now exports to the U.S.A. on a large scale in the same product areas, e.g. electronic consumer goods, as those in which it obtained licensing agreements with American firms. Overseas firms, for the above and other reasons, are becoming increasingly less keen to enter into licensing agreements, and it seems likely that Japan will have to rely to a lesser extent on this method of acquiring technological know-how. Japanese industry is now at the point where it will increasingly have to develop its own advanced technology.

We are not putting forward Japan as a model for other countries to follow, but Japanese experience does seem to emphasize, yet again, that technological innovation has to be regarded as an integrated process.

CHAPTER 10

The Effects of Technological Change

In this chapter and Chapter 11, we look at some of the effects of innovation. We have divided our discussion into two parts. In this chapter our approach is based upon an inter-industry analysis of the effects of technological change, as we are particularly interested in the effects on wages, profits, prices, and employment. In the next chapter, we look at the role of technological change in the growth of the economy as a whole. We have chosen not to discuss questions of pollution and the environmental aspects of technology, central as these are to the matter; our reasons are given in the Epilogue to the book.

RESEARCH AND DEVELOPMENT EXPENDITURES AND PRODUCTIVITY CHANGE

Innovations are made in order to produce new products, to modify existing products, or to make existing products in more efficient ways. As research and development expenditures are made by firms with the ultimate aim of producing an innovation, if follows that we might expect to see some systematic relationship between research and development expenditure and productivity growth, a relationship that would vary from industry to industry.

It is not easy to test this hypothesis for the U.K. over a long period as the earliest year for which research and development expenditures by industry are available is 1961. The time lags between expenditure and results are long and variable, as we have seen, and it is not clear which period of productivity growth should be used to trace cause and effect. Since about 1970, too, it seems that significant productivity growth has occurred because of changes in the manpower policies followed by firms.[1] In what follows we compare research and development expenditure, for 1961, as a percentage of net output in that year with the growth of output per man over the period 1963–70.

---

[1] This trend was discernible before 1970, but has become more developed since 1970.

The unemployment rate in these years was 2·6% and 3·4%, respectively, which is about as close as it is possible to get without drastically shortening the time period. Thus, to some extent, the two years were similar in the main, known, short term factor affecting productivity per man, the state of trade. The comparison is confined to manufacturing industry as private research and development activity outside manufacturing is negligible and there is, in any case, no available breakdown of such expenditure. The degree of aggregation is dictated by the research and development statistics. The results are presented in Table 10.1.

TABLE 10.1. *Research intensity and the Rate of Growth of Output per Man in U.K. Manufacturing Industry, 1963–70*

	R & D Expenditure as a Percentage of Net Output (1961)	Annual Percentage Rate of Growth of Output per Man (1963–70)
Food, drink and tobacco	0·8	1·9
Chemicals	6·7	6·2
Metal manufacture	1·3	2·0
Mechanical engineering, metal goods not elsewhere specified, shipbuilding	2·4	2·8
Electronics and telecommunications	18·6	6·3
Other electrical goods	9·0	5·3
Motor vehicles and railways	4·1	3·0
Aircraft	54·1	2·2
Textiles, leather and clothing	1·0	3·8
Bricks	1·4	3·3
Timber and paper	0·4	1·9
Other manufacturing	2·6	3·9

Sources: *Statistics of Science and Technology*, London, HMSO, 1967.
National Income and Expenditure, London, HMSO, 1970.
Department of Employment Gazette, London, HMSO, 1972.
Monthly Digest of Statistics, Central Statistical Office, 1972.

If we leave aside the aircraft industry for the moment, we can see that productivity in the research intensive industries increased faster than it did in the other manufacturing industries. The two groups of industries (food, and timber and paper) with the lowest research intensity, had the lowest rate of productivity growth. The odd man out is aircraft, with a very high research intensity and below average

130

productivity growth. Expenditure on research and development in this industry is largely financed by the government and non-economic considerations probably dominate. In what follows we omit the aircraft industry.

There was a statistical association between research intensity and productivity growth between 1963–70. This does not, of course, indicate a causal relationship. There are some theoretical grounds for expecting a causal link between research and development expenditures and productivity growth, but there are equally some reasons why we find it odd that such a relationship should be observable.

First, a significant proportion of research and development expenditures are devoted to the introduction of new products, and it is well known that conventional measures of output fail to capture the full impact of new products. More precisely, it has been argued that as new products are often introduced at higher relative prices than they sell for in the long run, and as price indices tend to under-represent new products, two biases will occur. First, the price indices will be biased upwards and hence real output will be biased downwards. Secondly, as prices of new products fall, and as they are increasingly reflected in price indices, an impression of productivity change is given when there is none.[1]

A second reason for expecting no close statistical relationship between research and development expenditures and productivity change is that the system of national income accounting fails to allow for quality change, and much research and development is aimed at improving the quality of products. Thus, when price increases are due in part to quality change, the price indices will in some sense be biased upwards and, correspondingly, real output and productivity change will be biased downwards.

Thirdly, we have already seen that many industries can improve their productivity through improvements in the intermediate goods they purchase. Much of the effect of research and development expenditure in the engineering industries, for example, will be felt as an improvement in the productivity of the user industries. Correlating research and development expenditures with productivity change in the same industry misses this inter-industry effect.

Fourthly, we have already emphasized that, to have any effect on output, much research and development must be embodied in plant and machinery. This complicates the time lags, because of the different rates of embodiment arising from the vintage models that we have already discussed, and makes the simple correlation between the two variables appear far too unsubtle. Differences in the speed

[1] W. Gustafson, 'Research and Development, New Products, and Productivity Change', *American Economic Review*, 1962.

131

with which embodiment occurs is a special case of a more general proposition, which states that the effects of innovation on productivity depend essentially on the extent to which, and the speed at which, the innovation is diffused. Thus, the whole complex of factors that we have discussed in connection with diffusion comes into play.

For these reasons, the fit observed in Table 10.1 seems too good to be true. Sargent has also looked at the association between research intensity and productivity growth.[1] He used the density of employment of qualified scientists and engineers (QSE), instead of research and development expenditures, as his measure of research activity, and he used total factor productivity instead of labour productivity. Sargent found no correlation between productivity and the QSE density by industry, in the two time periods he studied, 1955–60 and 1960–64. When only the science based industries were included in the sample, however, QSE density explained about one-half of the variance in total factor productivity.

A study in the U.S.A. has, however, produced more positive results.[2] Minasian tested the hypothesis that 'productivity increases are associated with investment in the improvement of technology and the greater the expenditures for research and development the greater the rate of growth of productivity'. He tested this hypothesis by using data on firms—eighteen firms in the chemicals industry and five drugs firms—over the period 1947–57. Obviously, this is more meaningful than our broad industrial categories. The productivity measure used was total factor productivity derived from a Cobb–Douglas production function. Surprisingly, high correlation coefficients of around 0·7 were obtained, and, interestingly enough, various other hypotheses (notably that productivity would be explained by gross investment) were apparently disproved. As the author points out, however, this was a strictly non-random sample and the results should not be generalized without further thought. There are good grounds for arguing that the chemical industry is, in this respect, not typical of industry as a whole.

Attempts to relate productivity growth with research and development expenditures seem to be very sensitive to the precise forms of the two variables that are used, the time period and the industrial breakdown, and to the industrial coverage that is used.

However, we can approach the question in another way which avoids some of the problems encountered earlier. It seems fairly safe for us, by this stage, to argue that technological change is caused by

[1] J. Sargent, 'The Distribution of Scientific Manpower'. Paper read to the International Economic Association Conference, 1971.
[2] J. Minasian, 'The Economics of Research and Development', in: *The Rate and Direction of Inventive Activity*, Princeton, Princeton University Press, 1962.

research and development expenditures. So, can we show that most productivity growth must be caused by technological change? The classic analysis of this question is that by Salter.[1]

Salter's sample covered twenty-eight industries (minimum list headings) selected on the basis of the availability of data. He collected various data on these industries for the years 1924–50. In an addendum to the second edition of the book, Salter's analysis has been extended by Reddaway to cover the years 1954–63. We have had made available to us a further extension, to 1968. In detail, the experience of these later periods seems to differ from that described by Salter, and we consider this later work in the next section. The basic result that we are interested in at this point, however, is confirmed by this subsequent work.

The change in productivity, measured by output per man, varied widely between one industry and another. The median increase in productivity between 1924 and 1950 was 51% with a large range on either side of this figure. The extreme cases were cutlery, where productivity increased by 212% and wallpaper, where there was an absolute decline of 16% in productivity. Various hypotheses can be put forward to explain the causes of changes in labour productivity. The personal efficiency of labour might have increased; labour might have acquired extra skills or knowledge; it might simply have worked harder.

But this sort of reasoning fails to explain the observed pattern of experience on three counts. First, it does not seem plausible that such large differences in personal efficiency would have occurred in different industries, although it is just possible that the more able workers might have moved to the more efficient trades. Secondly, there is no correlation between increases in output per head and increases in earnings, which one would expect if the productivity change was due to increased labour efficiency. Thirdly, it was observed that in the industries with the greatest increases in labour productivity there was a simultaneous fall, both in labour and non-labour costs. If labour grows more efficient, why should non-labour costs fall as well? While it is not denied that increases in labour efficiency made some contribution to the improvements in labour productivity, labour efficiency does not seem likely to have been a dominant force at work.

A second possible hypothesis is that labour productivity increased through a substitution of capital for labour. This is a more sophisticated explanation than the earlier one and it is likely to appeal to economists. It is based upon the notion that at any one point of time there is a series of blueprints of techniques. As relative factor prices change so production managers choose blueprints that make less use

[1] W. Salter, *op. cit.*, especially chs 8–10.

of the relatively more expensive factor. Given the pattern of earnings increases, it follows that differential increases in productivity are to be explained through inter-industry differences in the elasticity of substitution of capital for labour. Thus, where substitutability is relatively easy, capital inputs increase relative to labour; labour productivity consequently increases and unit capital costs rise. But—although there are some difficulties in finding the data—it appears that those industries with the greatest increases in labour productivity in fact experienced the smallest increases in unit capital costs. And if productivity change were primarily due to substitution we should expect little impact on relative prices. But relative prices have moved in an inverse direction to the differential increases in labour productivity.

A third explanation offered of the differences in productivity growth is that there are differential rates of technological change in different parts of the economy. This argument proceeds by a series of steps. First, we include improvements due to economies of scale in technological change. Science, as we have seen, varies in its impact on industry. New science based industries are continually being pushed along by advances in scientific knowledge. But in many industries this sort of impetus is absent. 'Young' industries are only beginning to exploit cost reductions due to economies of scale. As they proceed in this, then there will be further improvements in technological and scientific knowledge. Thus, Salter—whose theory this is—argues, as others have done, that economies of scale and technological change are complementary to each other, and holds that it is difficult to separate out their individual effects. It is certainly possible, Salter says, that these joint effects have been accompanied by some degree of factor substitution, induced by the increases in the price of labour relative to that of capital goods. But this relative decrease in the price of capital goods has been partially caused by technological advance in the capital goods industries. There is thus an additional interrelationship between technological change, economies of scale, gross investment, and productivity improvement.

The dominant influences on productivity change are, therefore, technological advance and the realization of scale economies. These two influences are very closely bound up. At the same time, of course, there have been other influences on labour productivity—among them increases in the personal efficiency of labour and a substitution of capital for labour. In so far as technological change and economies of scale are the dominant ones, however, the vehicle of productivity change is gross investment. Most technological change is of the 'embodied' sort and it follows, by definition, that it cannot have positive effects on output without positive investment. It is also a truism that the realization of economies of scale depends on investment taking place.

We have seen, then, that productivity change has occurred at different rates in different industries, and the most plausible explanation is that this has been due to technological advance.

Here we come to the real question. What caused this technological advance? Some advance is due to economies of scale which, in turn, produces further potential economies of scale. The rest must largely have been due to advances in scientific and technological knowledge. But these advances must be related to *some* past expenditures on research and development. Since the relationship between research expenditures and improvements in knowledge, on the one hand, and technological change and innovation, on the other, are only loosely spelt out, and since the rate of diffusion of innovation differs (and because there are other factors at work on productivity), we shall not always expect to see a close fit between any actual research and development expenditures and any actual productivity change. The relative importance of all these separate effects is not precisely known. It does seem likely, however, that there are strong interrelationships between them. So we see a complex pattern of relationships, dependent on many things, many of which we have examined in previous chapters.

THE EFFECTS ON WAGES, PROFITS AND PRICES

We now move on to examine the effects of technological change on things other than productivity, in particular the impact on employment, earnings and prices. The question is: who has captured the gains of productivity growth? Or, whom does technology benefit?

Three separate, extreme cases may be set out. First, if wage and salary earnings in each industry increased by the same percentage as productivity increased, then all of the gains would be captured by labour. There would be no scope for increased profit margins and relative prices would, *ceteris paribus*, remain constant. A second case would be that relative prices remain constant, and relative earnings between industries also remain constant. In this instance, the benefits of productivity growth would go to profits in the form of increased margins. Finally, we might envisage the case where relative earnings are constant, and where profit margins are unchanged. Here the full impact of differential productivity growth would be on relative prices. The products of those industries where productivity growth was rapid would decline in price relative to industries where the change in productivity was less. The consumers would gain. Between these three extreme possibilities, where all of the gains accrue to one group, there are, of course, a variety of possibilities.

Salter found that, in reality, the third case is correct, and that the main impact is on relative prices. Subsequent work has not fully confirmed this result. We begin by looking at Salter's results, which were for the period 1924–50.

First, let us look at the behaviour of relative earnings. One test would be whether relative earnings have altered much. The answer is that they did not do so over the period in question. The spread of earnings increases in 1924–50 was narrow, especially relative to the dispersion of productivity change.

There was no evidence that of the twenty-eight industries, shown in Table 10.2, those industries with the most rapid productivity growth also experienced the most rapid growth of wage earnings. In fact, the correlation between these two variables was approximately zero. It follows that unit labour costs fell more rapidly, the more rapid was the growth of output per man.

TABLE 10.2. *Changes over Period 1924–50: Twenty-eight Selected Industries*

	Output per Head	Earnings per Operative
Upper quartile	194	266
Median	151	250
Lower quartile	128	223

Source: W. Salter, *op. cit.*, p. 107.

Salter also found, however, that profits do not seem to take the benefit. If anything, reductions in unit gross margin cost accompanied reductions in unit labour costs.[1] Therefore, it follows that differential productivity growth must have been accompanied by changes in relative prices. And when we look at the evidence we see that in fact the statistical relationship is a correlation (r) of -0.88. The gains in productivity had, therefore, been distributed among the community as a whole and had not been appropriated at source either by labour or by the owners of firms, although clearly in individual cases certain groups may have been successful in appropriating some of the gains.

These relationships seem to have become much weaker in the years after 1950. It must be emphasized that the post-Salter work referred to is confined to the same twenty-eight industries. Although Salter checked for bias in his sample, and found none, it is not absolutely clear whether it is possible to apply the later results to the whole of industry. The twenty-eight industries which, with the

---

[1] Unit gross margin cost equals gross trading profit, including rent and interest payments.

exception of coal-mining and electricity are all in manufacturing, now account for rather less than 30% of industrial production.[1] There are, however, no good grounds for suspecting bias.

We have two sources of more recent analyses: Reddaway's Addendum to the second edition of Salter's work, which covers the period 1954–63; and results for an overlapping period, 1954–68, which have been calculated by one of our students.[2] The key results are presented in the form of coefficients of determination (R^2) in Table 10.3.

TABLE 10.3

	Time-period		
	(1924–50)	(1954–63)	(1954–58)
Coefficients of Determination between:			
1. Earnings and output per head	0	0	0·29
2. Price and output per head	0·77	0·29	0·16

The strong inverse relationship between prices and productivity movements appears to have progressively weakened. There is no evidence that unit gross margin costs have increased, so the cause of this change is that relative earnings in the later periods were related to different rates of growth of productivity.

Thus, the conclusion that the gains of technological change have generally been distributed to consumers still holds, but is no longer a very strong one. The major reason for this is that labour in industries where productivity growth has been relatively rapid have secured increases in their relative earnings. Why this change should have occurred is not clear.

That the community as a whole should receive some of the benefit from productivity change, has been implicit in various attempts at incomes policy in the U.K. and elsewhere. In 1967, for example, when the norm for pay increases was zero, an exception was made where workers had made a direct contribution towards productivity change, provided 'some of the benefit should accrue to the community as a whole'. Experience shows that at least some of the benefit has accrued to the whole community. In so far as most productivity change seems to arise from factors other than changes in the personal efficiency of labour, this seems a not inequitable outcome. Where the

[1] The industrial-production industries are manufacturing, mining, gas, electricity and water, and construction.
[2] D. Wharton, 'An Extension of the Research of W. E. G. Salter into the Relationship between Productivity and Technical Changing using Data for the Period 1954–68'. Degree dissertation, Brunel University, 1972.

efficiency of labour has increased, one would expect this to be reflected in earnings. Increased acquisition of skills by wage and salary earners in general has been reflected in increases in the real wages of most workers. We are concerned here only with changes in *relative* earnings and prices. Where dramatic changes in labour usage have to accompany technological change, organized labour is often in a position to be compensated. We discuss the effect of technological change upon employment in the final section of this chapter. Before doing this at a sectoral level, it is convenient to examine briefly the notion of the neutrality of technological change.

THE NEUTRALITY OF TECHNOLOGICAL CHANGE

Technological change alters the methods of production. What effect does this have on the relative usage of capital and labour? Those changes that, in some sense, leave the capital to labour ratio unaltered are described as 'neutral'. Unfortunately, at the same time as technological change occurs, or because of technological change, the level of output may be changing—so may the factor price ratio. For these reasons, there is no unambiguous definition of neutrality. There are, instead, various alternative proposals for definitions.

The questions of the neutrality of technological change can be treated either at an aggregative (national) level or at an industrial level. At the aggregate level, it is customary to talk of the neutrality (or non-neutrality) of *technical progress*, rather than of 'technological change'. In this context, the nature of technical progress is important in growth models where the possibility of steady state growth may depend crucially on the nature of technical progress. At this aggregate level, it is usual to restrict the discussion to cases where technical progress is disembodied, i.e. where it affects all machines, old and new alike, and where there is only one good. From a practical point of view, there seems little point in discussing such a world and our treatment will be very brief. It may enable us to focus on the points at issue, however.

The two definitions of neutrality most commonly used are those of Sir John Hicks and of Sir Roy Harrod. Hicks' neutrality obtains when, at a constant capital to labour ratio, technical progress leaves unchanged the ratio of the marginal productivity of capital to the marginal productivity of labour. Technical progress is said to be labour saving when (again at a constant capital to labour ratio) it reduces the ratio of the marginal product of labour to that of capital. Capital saving technical progress can be similarly defined. The problem with Hicks's criterion is that the capital to labour ratio is not usually constant, showing a secular tendency to increase. This difficulty is avoided on Harrod's criterion.

THE EFFECTS OF TECHNOLOGICAL CHANGE

Technical progress is neutral, according to Harrod, if, at a constant profit (interest) rate, the capital to output ratio is unchanged. On Harrod's definition technical progress is labour-saving, if, given the same profit rate, the capital–output ratio increases (and vice versa for capital saving technical progress).

Both criteria of neutrality yield the same result only in one special circumstance—when the elasticity of substitution between capital and labour is unity. That this is necessarily the case is best seen by examining the effect of technical progress on factor shares. Assume a constant labour force. If technical progress is Hicks neutral, then clearly the distribution of income must be unchanged, because at the same capital–labour ratio the ratio of the profit rate to the wage rate (as given by the respective marginal productivities, assuming perfect competition) remains unaltered. By Harrod neutrality, with a given labour force, at the same profit rate (π), the capital-output ratio (K/X) is constant. Thus, $\pi(K/X)$, which is capital's share of the national income, is constant. Thus, we are looking at two situations which have the same distribution and the same labour force, but in the latter the capital stock is greater. In the first case, the capital stock was constant; in the latter case it increased in the same proportion as output. With a constant labour force the two situations give the same distribution with different levels of the capital stock. Thus, the elasticity of substitution between capital and labour is unity, QED. The only production function which has a constant elasticity of substitution of unity over the whole of its range is the Cobb–Douglas production function, which partly explains its popularity in econometric work, where constant elasticity of unity is an immensely helpful simplifying assumption.

Unfortunately, once the assumption that the economy produces only one good is dropped, neither criterion remains unambiguous. Neither criterion is very useful for the analysis of technological change, or of innovation, at the industry level. This is most easily demonstrated in the case of Hicks's criterion. Hicks holds the ratio of capital to labour constant and examines the consequences on relative factor prices (marginal productivities). He assumes, in effect, that the productivity of both factors increases proportionately.[1] It is reasonable to assume factor *supplies* fixed in aggregate analysis, but not at the industry level. In studying an industry it is more realistic to hold relative factor *prices* constant, as they are not likely to be altered by changes in demand from one industry. We can then see the effect that technical progress has on the relative usage of capital and labour.

This is Salter's criterion. Formally, technological change is

[1] For Hicks neutrality, the production function is written $X = A(t) f (K,L)$. Technical progress (A) does not affect the form of the function.

neutral (unbiased) if, with constant relative factor prices, there is no change in the capital–labour ratio. Technological change has a labour saving bias if there is an increase in the capital–labour ratio and vice versa. This will give the same direction of change as Hicks's criterion, but not the same magnitude of change.

Harrod's scheme, like Hicks's, similarly is not suited to a dis-aggregative analysis, for Harrod looks at the net effect of at least two influences. First, there is the net result of technical advances in each individual industry. When change occurs in capital goods industries, or when technological change is relatively rapid in that sector, there is a cheapening of capital relative to labour. This leads, in turn, to an increase in the capital to labour ratio. This second influence affects all industries. It is more properly the result of changes in prices and it obscures the 'pure' technical advance in each industry which we have just discussed.

Salter argues that we should talk in terms of a technological change having a labour (capital) saving bias rather than being in itself labour (capital) saving. This is not quite like some of the distinctions drawn by the Early Christian Fathers, it has an important practical result. Many technological changes involve an absolute saving of both capital and labour, and so, if we talk of 'bias', we can emphasize this point. If a technique is labour saving, then those techniques which are labour intensive will have the greatest scope for yielding economies. Firms will have an incentive to switch to labour intensive techniques in order to take the greatest advantage of the change.

Formally the bias in a technical change is measured—on the assumption of constant relative factor prices—by B, where

$$B = \frac{d(K/L)}{dt}(L/K)$$

Where $B = 0$, technical change is neutral, where $B > 1$, technical change is labour saving biased, and where $B < 1$ technical change is capital saving biased.

LABOUR AND TECHNOLOGICAL CHANGE

We can discuss the impact of technological change on the employment of labour at three levels, namely, of the economy, of the industry, and at the level of the individual firm.

The effect of technological advance on the economy as a whole is to increase the production possibilities open to society. With a given amount of resources more can be produced. Yet, a traditional fear has been that the net effect of technological advance would be to increase unemployment. Marx and others taught that this would be so. And, indeed, it would be so, if the rate of growth of output were less than the rate of growth of output per man *plus* the rate of growth of the labour force. If we ignore for the moment what kinds of output are being produced and are increasing, and what sort of labour loses its jobs because of increased productivity, we can see that unemployment due to technological advance may be prevented by the proper management of the level of aggregate demand. This is Keynes's discovery.

The trouble is that, once we drop the assumption that output and labour are homogeneous, we have to face the fact that it may not be possible to reduce unemployment by expanding aggregate demand, because the unemployed may not possess the skills required by expanding industries. This has become known as the 'structural unemployment hypothesis'.

One of the best examples may be drawn from the coal industry where output per man has increased rapidly. Between 1957 and 1971, output per man-shift increased by 77·5%. We have seen that the main effect of rapid productivity change has generally been on relative prices. Though the price of coal has not risen as fast as prices in general, demand has nevertheless fallen, partly because the price of coal has not declined relative to the price of substitutes like oil and natural gas. The output of coal has fallen. This has compounded the effect on employment of the increase in output per man. Thus, employment in coal-mining has fallen considerably, from 700,000 in 1957 to 290,000 in 1971. But let us assume that the government adopts the policy of keeping aggregate demand rising in line with productive potential. The major impact of the expansion of aggregate demand will be felt by those industries whose products have high income elasticities of demand and by those industries whose prices are relatively decreasing, and whose products have high price elasticities of demand. These industries will therefore tend to offer increasing numbers of jobs. They are the leisure trades and service occupations like banking and insurance.

Ideally, the unemployed miners would take these jobs. But, of course they do not usually possess the necessary skills to do so and they do not live in the right places. The expanding trades and industries are largely located in different regions from where the unemployed live.

Structural unemployment calls for different cures than does demand deficiency unemployment. The cure will differ from case to case. Where structural unemployment is concentrated regionally, then some form of regional policy aimed at varying the industrial mix of high unemployment regions is called for. A discussion of regional policy would be outside the scope of this book, but it is obvious that in the U.K., and in many countries, the regional unemployment problem has proved a very stubborn one.

Regional policies have in any case to be backed up by attempts to retrain men and women in new skills. Younger people tend to be retrained by new employers, but for older people the chances of adequate training are small. In cases where industries decline slowly, the burden of decline can be taken by voluntary retirements and by a decline in the hiring rate. Although this reduces redundancies, the unemployment problem remains as long as the declining industry is localized.

But there is a brighter side to the picture of unemployment caused by technology. Much technological change takes the form of breaking down an operation into smaller and simpler parts. Skill requirements may be relatively easy to acquire. In the Coventry high earnings engineering industry, for example, most men receive only two weeks' training compared with the conventional four-year engineering apprenticeship. But many new job opportunities arise in factories. Factory work is, however, often anathema to men who have worked in agriculture, shipbuilding, mining, and some other declining industries. This is a problem that no amount of retraining can overcome.

The balance of the argument seems to be that the more extreme form of the structural unemployment hypothesis can be rejected, but that there is a permanent problem. The general outlines of the solution are well known, but, especially where structural unemployment is localized, it may be difficult to administer the necessary policies. In all of this argument, too, we must not lose sight of the very real human costs of change. There may be generous redundancy payments, unemployment-pay, and the subsidization of retraining schemes, but the death of old cultures and communities is not to be measured in financial terms.

To ascribe all structural unemployment directly to technological advance would, of course, be absurd. Differential rates of growth of different industries are caused by such factors as differing income elasticities of demand, changes in tastes and changes in factor availability. Many of the employment effects of technological change are, in any case, indirect. Employment in industries themselves experiencing no technological change, will be positively effected by technological advances in industries producing complementary goods and negatively affected by advances in industries producing substitutes.

When we look at any industry in detail we are concerned in this connection with whether technological advance will have a positive or negative effect on employment in that industry. The net effect on employment will be compounded of three separate tendencies: first, whether the technological change is labour saving biased or capital saving biased (Salter thought that technological change had been roughly neutral overall); secondly, the reduction in total cost that results from an increase in labour productivity; and thirdly, the reaction of demand (output) to any consequent change in relative prices. The second effect will normally reduce employment (same output can be produced with fewer men), while the third effect will normally operate to expand output. In the industries covered by Salter's survey, from 1924–50, the expansive effect tended to be the stronger. There was a positive correlation (0·61) of changes in output per head with employment. An industry experiencing a 10% *differential* increase in output per man would on average gain a 6–7% *differential* increase in employment.

Studies based on other data have not reached the conclusion that technological change leads to an increase in employment in the same industry. Salter found in a sample of twenty-seven industries in the U.S.A. that the correlation between changes in output per man hour and man-hours worked was approximately zero. This conclusion roughly agrees with that of Kendrick.[1] When Reddaway extended Salter's analysis to the 1954–63 period he found that the U.K. experience in that period conformed to the U.S. pattern, as it did also between 1954–68.[2]

These rather negative results at least dispel the spectre of large-scale, technological unemployment. Particular industries will, as we have seen, experience large declines in employment along with large increases in labour productivity, which again emphasizes the need for policies to facilitate transfer.

Finally, society may choose to take some of the benefits of technological advance in the form of increased leisure, rather than in more or less employment in terms of jobs. Over long periods of time there has been a gradual decline in average hours worked, a decline which has continued in recent decades. Over the period 1956–70, the average weekly hours worked by manual workers fell by 6%, from 46·7 hours to 43·9 hours. This decline was less than that in 'normal' hours of work, i.e. the number of hours that are paid at standard, rather than overtime, rates of pay. Normal hours declined by 9·6% from 44·6 hours to 40·3 hours.

When we consider the impact of technological change on the individual firm's employees we must be careful to distinguish

[1] J. Kendrick, *Productivity Trends in the United States*, Economic National Bureau of Research, Princeton, 1961.

[2] Over the period 1954–68, a regression of total employment on output per head shows a negative relationship. Over the period 1954–63 the relationship was positive. In neither case, however, is the regression coefficient statistically significant.

between those cases where the firm is directly influenced by techno-logical change and those where the firm is indirectly influenced. In the former category, we include the firms who introduce the change; and in the latter, firms who are influenced by these changes. It seems that any adverse effects of technological change on labour are much greater in the indirect case. Let us consider first a firm planning to change its pattern of production—or method of production—in order to take advantage of a new technique. Let us further assume that this means that the firm faces an excess stock of at least some grades of labour. The firm can *plan* how to cope with this excess stock, because it will have control over the timing of the innovation and the precise way in which the innovation occurs. The knowledge of a forthcoming surplus enables the firm to allow natural wastage to occur. Employees leaving the firm are, in general, not replaced. The problem of any remaining excess of labour can be approached in one or more of three ways, through redundancies, redeployment or resettlement. The optimum choice of method may be made by balancing the marginal returns and costs from each, but it seems likely that choices are not made entirely, or even largely, on such a basis. Contractual and institutional constraints are operative—e.g. 'no redundancy' clauses may have been negotiated with unions, and craft unions may not accept the employment of retrained men. Employees may, in other ways, not act as passive agents when such decisions are being considered, or the firm may independently choose not to act on financial grounds alone. In a recent study of the effects of technological change in large and progressive companies with expanding output—in chemicals, steel and printing—it emerged that resettlement, which is defined as employment at another plant beyond daily travelling distance of the affected plant, was relatively unim-portant and redundancies were seen as a last resort.[1] Thus, the main burden of change was carried through redeployment, although there is some evidence that the Redundancy Payments Act, 1965, has increased the willingness of both unions and employers to use redundancies—especially of older workers—as a means of adjust-ment.

We have seen that differential rates of technological advance lead to relative (product) price changes with the result that, although the impact effect is to reduce labour requirements, there is often a secondary positive effect on employment. The effect may or may not operate to increase employment to its original level or above. In any event, a firm may be willing to 'carry' some surplus labour until the expected increase in output materializes. This will be especially true,

[1] L. Hunter, G. Reid and D. Boddy, *Labour Problems of Technological Change*, London, Allen & Unwin, 1970.

of course, where the men possess specific skills that will be needed later, and in areas of high demand for labour. In the case of craft workers, the most important form of retraining in the firms studied was not the acquisition of a new craft but the 'acquisition of new techniques within the craft or the ability to work with new materials'. Training in a new craft is costly and there is often restriction of entry into skilled trades. For production workers, as we have noted earlier, there is less of a problem as the necessary skills are relatively easy to acquire and on-the-job training is normally sufficient.

Hunter, Reid and Boddy further suggest that manning standards do not always reflect the potential of new equipment. There is no blueprint which gives the required number of men for a new piece of equipment—or a new plant—and it is difficult to derive optimum labour requirements, especially in complex plants. There is always a bias towards overmanning; undermanning will quickly be brought to the notice of management. They suggest three main reasons for a tendency to overmanning. Additional men (over estimated require-ments) will be employed in the running-in period of a new plant—to cope with unforeseen problems, ensure that the whole plant is operating correctly, and so on. The danger is that at least some of this overmanning remains long after the running-in problems have been solved. Much technological change, as we have emphasized, takes the form of many small improvements, rather than significant advances. Each small change may not warrant a reduction in em-ployment, but in total, over a period of time, they may imply a reduction in manning requirements. Unless this is perceived, over-manning may build up over time. Also, depending on the weight they give to protection of employment as a goal, unions may through the negotiation of 'no redundancy' clauses, delays, and the negotiation of lax manning standards cause new plants to be overmanned. The success of unions in achieving this will depend among other things on the amount of competition in the product market and the import-ance of labour costs in total costs. As an example of overmanning, we may quote Guinness, the brewers, who found that in 1970 their Dublin brewery employed over twice the ideal number of workers by optimum technological standards. The whole problem of overmanning can be approached through productivity bargaining, but it is not possible to discuss bargaining here.[1]

Innovation by one firm, however, has an impact on other firms. Innovating firms will tend to expand their output and increase their market share. Thus, other firms—those producing substitutes for example—may have to decrease their output. The effects on their

---

[1] For a general discussion of manning standards, productivity bargaining, and labour force adjustment, see L. Hunter, G. Reid and D. Boddy, *op. cit.*, chs 11–13.

employment of labour may be adverse, and there will be fewer alternative means of adjustment available to them. A firm experiencing a contraction of output will not be able to redeploy or resettle labour and the main burden of adjustment will have to be carried by redundancies. Such firms will have little control over the timing of redundancies and, accordingly, will not be able to plan redundancies. Also they will often not be in a position to be generous to redundant labour. Men who feel the impact of technological change in this way, then, will face serious problems. There is a strong case for government intervention, but this has not been completely successful and structural unemployment must be counted as one of the costs of technological change.

CHAPTER 11

Technology and Growth

It was evident in the nineteenth century that the rapid advances in technological knowledge that occurred in Western Europe must have been an important cause of the growth of output, and output per head. Yet it was not until the 1950s that economists began to pay systematic attention to the role of technology in growth. The upsurge of interest dates from empirical work which seemed to show that increases in factor inputs could not explain even the major part of increases in output.

This is not a textbook on economic growth, but changes in technology are so closely bound up with the growth of aggregate output that we must devote some attention to growth. We have no need to build or examine complex models, because we are primarily concerned with the role that technology is seen to play in growth, and more particularly with empirical estimates of the importance of this role. Despite this, the material in this chapter tends to be somewhat detached from the realism of the rest of the book.

Most of the work that we shall consider has aimed at isolating the importance of technological change in economic growth, rather than attempting to relate research and development expenditures to the rate of growth. We explained our position on this in the previous chapter. Most technological change must be related to some research and development activity, but it does not seem in general possible to indicate in which time-period the relevant activity occurred or in which country. We shall mostly be concerned with studies based upon some form of aggregate production function. To deal with these we will obviously have to assume the existence of an aggregate production function. We will look more closely at this assumption later.

It is suggested that by distinguishing between moves along, and shifts in, the production function, it is possible to divide the sources of growth into two parts: increases in factor inputs, and increases in output per unit of inputs. Increases in output, which are not due to increases in inputs, are referred to as 'technical progress'. *Anything*

147

which increases the output per unit of factor inputs is technical progress. Hence, technical progress has nothing necessarily to do with research, or inventions, or changes in technology. Technical progress encompasses a multitude of influences upon the growth of output. All of that part of output which cannot be attributed to the growth of the inputs in the aggregate production function is termed technical progress. It is evident that measures of technical progress are, therefore, very sensitive to the methods used to measure the inputs in the production function. Thus, issues which will concern us include the problem of measuring the capital stock, the labour force and the extent to which technological change has to be embodied in new capital equipment before it has any positive effect on output. As an empirical development of this approach there exists work which seeks to break down this residual item (technical progress) into several component parts, some of which are technological factors.

A second view of technical progress in growth denies the distinction between shifts in, and moves along, an aggregate production function. Those using this approach do not accept that it is meaningful to talk in terms of such a function, since it does not exist. As an alternative, a form of technical progress function is used. We will briefly look at this approach.

We shall conclude by indicating a view of the role of technological change in growth which seems to us to emerge from the arguments and facts that we have presented in all the previous chapters of this book.

THE AGGREGATE PRODUCTION FUNCTION APPROACH: SOLOW

In traditional economic theory there are three factors of production. In a developed economy, land is usually assumed not to impose any restrictions on production and it is convenient to drop land as a factor. We are thus left with two factors, labour and capital.

At the level of the firm it is postulated that, for each firm, there exists a production function which, for any combination of inputs of capital (K) and labour (L) defines a unique output (Q). Thus:

$$Q = F(K,L)$$

The relationship is basically an engineering one and can be seen as being defined by the existing technology. If such a relationship exists for each firm, it is tempting to suppose that we could aggregate this relationship for all firms, and for all industries, to derive an aggregate production function for the whole economy. Thus, Q

would become national output, K the aggregate capital stock, and L the employed labour force. In fact, such aggregation is only formally possible under certain conditions, but we shall defer discussion of these until later in the chapter. Before discussing the properties and uses of aggregate production functions, we must first look at how we are to measure the inputs and output in such functions. For, unfortunately, the matter is less easy than would appear at first sight and, in fact, poses severe problems.

In theoretical work it is possible to avoid problems in measuring outputs and inputs by assuming, for example, that there is only one good (say corn) which can be used either as a consumption good or as a capital good (seed corn). In empirical work, of course, this sort of escape route is closed and the measurement problems arising from the heterogeneity of inputs and outputs have to be faced. The multitude of physical outputs can be brought down to a single monetary measure, such as GNP, by using prices. The time series of output is thus some aggregate output concept, at constant prices. As we have seen, conventional measures of output fail to allow fully for changes in the quality of goods produced and we must return to this problem.

Labour inputs are usually measured in terms of men or in manhours: thus the quality of labour is implicitly assumed to be unchanged over time. The main problem variable is capital. As with output, a method has to be found to add all the heterogeneous physical units together to derive a single figure for the capital stock of the economy in each year. The difficulty is that to be of any use the measure of the aggregate capital stock has to be independent of variations in interest rates, profit rates, wage rates, and the pace of technological advance. To see the effect of these variables, let us consider two ways of looking at the capital stock.

First, the forward view. Here the value of a capital good is equal to the net discounted present value of the stream of future receipts due to the capital good. These receipts are the revenues assigned to the good when the costs of all other associated inputs have been deducted. Such estimates can only be undertaken when, among other things, the future rate of technological change is known or can be estimated. For the faster the rate of technological change, the smaller will be the stream of net receipts. This is because, in the future, newer machines will become available which, as they are installed in production, will reduce the quasi-rents earned on the old machines (see Ch. 7). Thus, estimates of the capital stock will only be valid as long as the rate of technological advance occurs at the projected rate. Similarly, changes in the other variables will alter estimates. For example, if the wage rates increases then the net receipts from the capital good will (other things being equal) fall, the more so if in future other firms use techniques that are less labour intensive. Thus, estimates of the capital stock would have to be continually revised as conditions changed.

On an alternative view, the capital stock is equal to the sum of investments that have taken place in the past less an allowance for depreciation. Thus, consider two machines, one just purchased for £1,000, and the other purchased last year (assuming a constant price level) for £1,000. If the more recent machine embodies more up-to-date technology, then in some sense it represents 'more' capital. So, how is last year's machine valued? It is worth less for two reasons: it will have physically deteriorated, and also deteriorated economically, because subsequent machines are more efficient. This latter deterioration could be measured, but it is not possible to allow for next year's deterioration (of either machine), unless the rate of technological progress, profit rates, etc., are known. In practice, allowances for obsolescence are based on accounting conventions—typically, a length of life (n years) is assumed and the value of the machine is reduced by $1/n$ each year. The lengths of life used for different sorts of equipment is often based on the current tax law and are thus subject to arbitrary changes. Although we can argue that these 'assumed' lives of different machines would be altered if they were proved to be continually incorrect, it seems most unlikely that the valuation of capital equipment by firms corresponds in any but the crudest sense to the correct economic valuation. Yet published figures have, at least partially, to be based on estimates made by firms.

In the *National Accounts Statistics* of the U.K., estimates of the capital stock are based on the perpetual inventory method, which corresponds to the second method described above. The precise method used is summarized as follows: 'Estimates or assumptions are made about the average length of life of each class of asset separately distinguished. Gross fixed capital formation is then estimated for each class of asset for L years prior to Y, where L is the average life of the class of asset in question and Y is the year for which capital consumption and the gross stock are to be estimated. Price indices are applied to these estimates to convert them to constant prices. The estimates at constant prices are then aggregated for L years to obtain the estimate of the capital stock. Division of the capital stock by L gives the estimate of capital consumption at constant prices. The price indices are then used to convert to whatever price basis is required.'[1] Figures for net capital stock, that is the gross capital stock less accrued capital consumption, are presented by

[1] *National Accounts Statistics: Sources and Methods*, London, HMSO, 1968, p. 384.

sector and type of asset, and gross capital stock estimates are given for broad industrial groups. It is emphasized that neither the net nor the gross estimates of the capital stock make any allowance for technological change. This is basically because capital consumption should be calculated from the cost of replacing capacity, whereas it is based on the cost of replacing assets with identical assets. As they stand, the estimates of the aggregate capital stock are thought to have a reliability of plus or minus 10–20%, although for many individual industries the reliability is even less.

The estimates of technical progress made by Solow and Denison that we discuss below were based on historic cost estimates of the capital stock.

We now return to our discussion of the aggregate production function. We had that:

$$Q = F(K,L) \tag{1}$$

It is usual to assume that the function is continuous and twice differentiable. In economic terms this means that the units of labour and capital are divisible into infinitely small units and are continuously substitutable for each other.[1] The first partial derivatives of this function give the marginal productivities of capital ($\partial Q/\partial K$) and labour ($\partial Q/\partial L$). The marginal productivity of labour is defined as the change in output due to an infinitely small change in labour input, all other factors being constant; partially differentiating the function with respect to labour gives just this.

A particular form of aggregate production function plays a crucial role in neo-classical economics. This is the form that exhibits constant returns to scale. If a production function has constant returns to scale and if both inputs are simultaneously increased by some proportion then output will increase in the same proportion. If this holds true everywhere the function is linear and homogeneous of degree one. This is important for neoclassical economics because a property of such functions is:

$$Q = \frac{\partial Q}{\partial K} K + \frac{\partial Q}{\partial L} L \tag{2}$$

As ($\partial Q/\partial K$) is the marginal product of capital, and *if* factors are paid their marginal products, then ($\partial Q/\partial K$)K is the total payment to capital and similarly ($\partial Q/\partial L$)L is the total payment of labour. Thus, total payments to the two factors just exhaust the product. We shall see, oddly enough, that this result is of some importance in interpreting the role in growth of technological change.

---

[1] This is not quite such a restrictive assumption as it appears at first sight. Substitution can take the form of product or process substitution.

If the aggregate production function has constant returns to scale we can rewrite equation (1) as

$$\frac{Q}{L} = F\left(\frac{K}{L}, 1\right) \qquad (3)$$

Using our assumptions, this enables us to show the function in diagrammatic form (see Fig. 11.1).

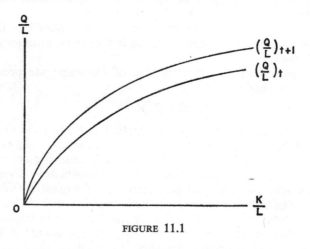

FIGURE 11.1

The function Q_t shows how output per man will increase as capital per man is increased, in the absence of technical progress. The function is drawn as concave from below, and this curvature shows diminishing returns to capital, labour inputs being fixed.

Now, how do we show the effect of technical progress on this diagram? In the simplest case, we make two assumptions about the nature of technical progress. First, that it is 'disembodied' and thus favourably affects the output of old and new machines alike—i.e. it does not have to be embodied in new capital equipment. An example of disembodied technical progress would be an improvement in the skills of production managers, enabling them without capital expenditure to increase the output per unit input of their plants. Secondly, assume that the rate of technical progress is exogenously determined and hence is not influenced by the level of any other economic variable—it 'falls like manna from heaven'.

On these assumptions the effect of technical progress is to shift the aggregate production function upwards, as in Figure 11.1. Thus if $(Q/L)_t$ was the position of the function at time $_t$, the technical progress occurring in the next period shifts the function to the position represented by $(Q/L)_{t+1}$. Thus, for any given level of capital per man, output per man has increased. The precise form of the vertical shift is determined by the nature of the technical progress. That is, it depends on whether it is neutral or non-neutral and on the definition of neutrality that is used.

To use this sort of approach to calculate the amount of technical progress that has occurred, it is necessary to fit an aggregate production function to time series data. In fitting a function there is, of course, an identification problem. For at the same time as the capital accumulation is occurring which causes moves *along* the production function, technical progress is *shifting* the function.

One of the earliest examples, which stimulated much of the subsequent work, was the attempt by Solow to estimate technical progress in the U.S.A., between 1909 and 1949.[1] Solow uses a function of the form:

$$Q = A(t)f(K,L) \qquad (4)$$

Here, $A(t)$ is a 'shift' factor, to allow for technical progress which is assumed to be disembodied, and neutral in the sense that it does not alter the marginal rate of substitution between capital and labour.[2]

Differentiating equation (4) with respect to time and denoting time-derivatives by dots gives:

$$\frac{\dot{Q}}{Q} = \frac{\dot{A}}{A} + A\frac{\partial f}{\partial K}\frac{\dot{K}}{Q} + A\frac{\partial f}{\partial L}\frac{\dot{L}}{Q} \qquad (5)$$

Now, $(\partial f/\partial K)K/Q$ is equal to capital's share of total output, which we denote by W_k, and similarly for labour's share, W_l. Substituting in equation (5) and re-arranging gives:

$$\frac{\dot{Q}}{Q} = \frac{\dot{A}}{A} + W_k\frac{\dot{K}}{K} + W_l\frac{\dot{L}}{L} \qquad (6)$$

Equation (6) states that the rate of growth of output is equal to the rate of technical progress $(\dot{A}/A)$ plus the rate of increase of inputs, each input being weighted by its share in the national income. This equation can be reduced further, and put into a form consistent with Figure 11.1, by utilizing the assumption that there are constant returns

[1] R. Solow, 'Technical Change and the Aggregate Production Function', *Review of Economics and Statistics*, 1957.

[2] Solow's neutral technical progress has the same properties as does Harrod's neutral technical progress, which was discussed in Chapter 10, with K and L reversed. Thus, technical progress is Solow neutral, if at a constant wage rate the labour to output ratio is unchanged.

to scale and that factors of production are paid their marginal products. For then the factor shares must sum to unity, and thus $W_l = 1 - W_k$. Denoting Q/L by q and K/L by k, then, as

$$\frac{\dot{q}}{q} = \frac{\dot{Q}}{Q} - \frac{\dot{L}}{L}$$

equation (6) can be written as:

$$\frac{\dot{q}}{q} = \frac{\dot{A}}{A} + W_k \frac{\dot{k}}{k} \qquad (7)$$

Technical progress, thus, emerges as a residual, being the rate of growth of output per head less the rate of growth of the capital stock per man weighted by the proportionate share of profit in the national income.

Solow fitted equation (7) to U.S. data for the period 1909–49. His results show that of the increase in output per head only 12·5% was due to increased capital per man, leaving no less than 87·5% of the growth rate as being due to technical progress.

At first sight this seems a very surprising result, for its implication is that if capital per man had remained constant over the forty years, output per head in the U.S.A. would still have increased by 87·5% of the increase that took place. Essentially, this is due to the assumption that technical progress is disembodied. Once technical progress has to be embodied in new machines and other capital equipment, before it can be taken advantage of, the role of investment in growth increases.

Solow has since developed a vintage model in which each machine embodies the technology of its vintage. The effect is to increase the significance of investment. Some subsequent work has followed this path, but we shall not pursue it further. We may note in passing, however, that a difficulty faced by models with embodied technical progress is that, to get an estimate of technical progress, the capital stock series has to be adjusted for the rate of technical progress. Since this cannot be done until the rate of technical progress is known, some iterative procedure has to be followed.

We now consider the work of Denison. Denison's method is set in the same framework as Solow's original work but attempts to break up the residual into its component parts. This is more promising from our point of view. Instead of being left only with the 'catch-all' that is termed technical progress, we may hopefully progress towards identifying the contribution to growth made by advances in science and technology.

154

THE AGGREGATE PRODUCTION FUNCTION APPROACH: DENISON

The most comprehensive empirical work on the explanation of growth rates and the analysis of technical progress is that of Denison.[1] This is a monumental piece of research and it will not be possible here to do full justice to its scope and detail. To clear the way to a discussion, and assessment, of the results, however, it is important that we examine the theoretical foundation of Denison's approach. The foundations are, in fact, implicit, for Denison does not discuss aggregate production functions, although all of his results are based on assumptions of the nature of such a production function.

The essence of the aggregate production function approach was reflected in equation (6) above, that is:

$$\frac{\dot{Q}}{Q} = \frac{\dot{A}}{A} + W_k \frac{\dot{K}}{K} + W_l \frac{\dot{L}}{L}$$

Denison takes this two stages further. First, he carries out adjustments to the rather simple measures of factor inputs that Solow, for example, used. Denison's labour input has, for example, a quality adjustment. The measure of technical progress $(\dot{A}/A)$ that Denison arrives at thus differs from Solow's. Secondly, and this is the distinctive contribution, his main task was to break down technical progress into several component parts.

By using factor shares in weighting factor inputs, Denison is applying the marginal productivity theory of distribution, and implicitly uses a Cobb–Douglas production function of the form:

$$Q = AL^\alpha K^{1-\alpha} \qquad (8)$$

The factor shares in such a function are the exponents. Further, each exponent gives the elasticity of output with respect to the relevant factor. Thus, if $\alpha = 0.75$, then a 1% increase in labour input would increase output by 0.75%. It is easy to see why on these assumptions factor shares are the relevant weights. That the factor shares are given by the exponents of the production function can be shown as follows. Partially differentiating equation (8) with respect to labour, gives the marginal product of labour:

$$\frac{\partial Q}{\partial L} = \alpha AL^{\alpha-1} K^{1-\alpha}$$

[1] There are several works. References here are to E. Denison, assisted by J. Poullier, *Why Growth Rates Differ*, Washington, Brookings Institution, 1967; London, Allen & Unwin, 1968.

Total payments to labour are the wage, which equals the marginal product of labour, multiplied by the number of workers employed. Thus, multiplying by L,

$$L\frac{\partial Q}{\partial L} = L\alpha A L^{\alpha-1} K^{1-\alpha}$$

$$= \alpha A L^{\alpha} K^{1-\alpha}$$

$$= \alpha Q$$

Labour's share in the national income (Q) is thus α. It can similarly be shown that the share of capital is $1 - \alpha$. To use the Cobb–Douglas, production function approach it is, therefore, not necessary actually to fit the function. All that is necessary is to calculate the factor shares from national income data. This is the reason that, in using these shares as weights, Denison implicitly employs an aggregate production function of the Cobb–Douglas type.

A final, methodological point remains to be made before we look at Denison's results. Since the factor shares sum to one, it follows from our earlier discussion that the production function exhibits constant returns to scale.

Although Denison is principally concerned with comparisons between countries, we present in Table (11.1) his results for the U.K. from 1950–62.

It may be helpful to relate this back to the fundamental equation

$$\frac{\dot{Q}}{Q} = \frac{\dot{A}}{A} + W_k\frac{\dot{K}}{K} + W_l\frac{\dot{L}}{L}$$

This states that the rate of growth of output is equal to technical progress plus the weighted rates of growth of labour and capital. Denison's results for the U.K. are:

$$2 \cdot 29 = 1 \cdot 18 + 0 \cdot 51 + 0 \cdot 60$$

Let us now briefly consider Table 11.1. The increase in the input of labour is made up of two component parts. One part is the change in the quantity of labour, which is given by the growth of employment adjusted for reductions in weekly hours of work and for changes in the age–sex composition of the labour force. The second part is the improvement in the quality of labour. This improvement is due to education. The calculation of the contribution of education is based on some very strong assumptions, and we have argued elsewhere that the resulting figure may not be very meaningful.[1] We should note,

---

[1] J. Vaizey, K. Norris and J. Sheehan, *op. cit.*, chs 3, 5.

TABLE 11.1. *U.K.: Sources of Growth of National Income and National Income per Person Employed, 1950–62*

Source of Growth	National Income	National Income per Person Employed
1. *National Income*	2·29	1·63
2. *Total Factor Input*	1·11	0·45
(a) *Labour Input*	0·60	0·10
Employment	0·50	—
Hours of work	−0·15	−0·15
Age–sex composition	−0·04	−0·04
Education	0·29	0·29
(b) *Capital Input*	0·51	0·37
Dwellings	0·04	0·02
International assets	−0·05	−0·06
Non-residential structures and equipment	0·43	0·35
Inventories	0·09	0·06
(c) *Land Input*	0·00	−0·02
3. *Output per Unit of Input*	1·18	1·18
(a) *Changes in Lag in Application of Knowledge, General Efficiency*	0·03	0·04
(b) *Improved Allocation of Resources*		
Contraction of agricultural inputs	0·06	0·06
Contraction of self-employment	0·04	0·04
Reduction of trade barriers	0·02	0·02
(c) *Economies of Scale*		
Growth of national market	0·22	0·22
Income elasticities	0·09	0·09
Independent growth of local markets	0·05	0·05
(d) *Irregularities in Pressure of Demand*	−0·09	−0·09
(e) *Advances of Knowledge*	0·76	0·75

Source: E. Denison, *op. cit.*, p. 314.

here, that most authors who calculate technical progress in this way do not adjust the labour inputs for quality change, and thus the resulting figure of technical progress is larger, because all of the effect of education goes into the residual.

The calculations of capital input are based, as we have said, on a historic-cost series of the capital stock. Denison calculates that, on this basis, increases in the capital stock contributed 0·51% to the growth of output.

Denison now proceeds to break down the increase in output per unit of input. The item which concerns us is the final one: advances in knowledge. In the U.K., the most important of the other sources of growth seems to have been the realization of economies of scale. In similar calculations for some other Western European countries, the shift of resources out of agriculture was found to be relatively important.

The estimate of the contribution of advances in knowledge comes out as a final residual. Let it be emphasized that there is no—and in this context there could not be—independent measure of the contribution to growth of advances in knowledge. Thus, the figure for advances in knowledge also includes 'the net effect of errors in the growth rates themselves, of errors in estimates of the contributions made by other sources of growth, and of omission of all sources not specifically specified'. It is clear, as the author acknowledges, that the estimate of the contribution made by advances in knowledge is the least reliable estimate in Table 11.1. We must remember, too, that technological change has often led to new or better final products. We have seen that the system of national accounts is unable to capture these benefits and, hence, necessarily they cannot be included in Denison's estimates.

As it stands, the result is that, in the U.K., advances in knowledge accounted for about one-third of the growth of output, and for nearly one-half of the growth of output per head. What are we to make of these figures?

All of the estimates are valid only as long as the approach is valid. The approach can be questioned on various levels and, although we do not want to dwell on this, it is important in assessing the estimate of advances in knowledge at least to note the objections. To begin with, it is objected that production functions of firms cannot be aggregated to produce a function for the economy as a whole. The conditions under which the production possibilities of an advanced industrial economy can be represented by an aggregate production function are very severe, and are not fulfilled in practice.[1] Secondly,

[1] F. Fisher, 'The Existence of Aggregate Production Functions', *Econometrica*, 1969.

the estimates depend upon the use of the marginal productivity theory of distribution.[1] Thirdly we must refer the reader back to the discussion on the measurability of capital. Denison has to use an historic-cost based capital series which cannot take into account technical change. He recognizes that, if the capital stock could be measured so as to reflect the contribution made by each machine to output in any given year, then the measured capital stock would grow faster as machines of later vintages embody more technological change. This would reduce the contribution of advances in knowledge. There is a further reason why the method used may underestimate the role of capital formation. This is that capital formation may induce learning, and hence technological change. We consider this view shortly.

There seem to be, then, some fairly fundamental objections to the overall approach. Even if we are willing to accept Denison's approach, the fact remains that advances in knowledge are the ultimate residual and reflect all other errors in the calculation. Many of the individual estimates are based on Denison's personal intuition, and while there is nothing to prove his intuition is wrong, there is nothing equally to prove that he is right. For example, Denison suggests that the U.K. economy operates under increasing returns to scale, such that a 1% proportionate increase in the use of labour and capital leads to a 1·1% increase in output. Apart from the obvious point that this is inconsistent with the use of the marginal productivity theory of distribution, there is no evidence that it represents the magnitude of economies of scale in the U.K. So, we are left with a residual item which, although termed 'advances in knowledge', constitutes, in fact, all advances in productivity that cannot be imputed to some other source.

Why Growth Rates Differ is a massive piece of research which breaks new ground in many places. As such it is very easy to be critical. Yet, the fact remains that Denison has produced an estimate of the contribution of 'advances in knowledge', and it is the only one we have. It has been suggested that critics who hold that (say) advances in knowledge have not contributed 0·76 percentage points to the growth rate should be challenged to say how much they think it has contributed. The point is well taken as long as one is willing to accept that it is a sensible question to ask in the first place. It

[1] The marginal productivity theory of distribution predicts constancy of factor shares in national income. An interesting result, recently derived, is that labour's share is not roughly constant because the Cobb–Douglas production function summarizes the economy's production possibilities, but rather that it is a good summary because labour's share is roughly constant. See F. Fisher, 'Aggregate Production Functions and the Explanation of Wages: a Simulation Experiment', *Review of Economics and Statistics*, 1971.

seems to us that the theoretical basis of Denison's work is open to too many criticisms for this final estimate to be accepted.

To show the rather arbitrary nature of the estimates of technical progress, or of technological change, that emerge from production function analysis we may refer to the work of Jorgenson and Griliches.[1]

Denison arrived at a smaller residual than did Solow because of the adjustments he made to labour inputs. It is possible to follow this approach further by attempting quality adjustments to the previously crude measures of all inputs. This is what has been done by Jorgenson and Griliches. They start from the proposition that, from a social accounting point of view, real product is equal to real factor input and, hence, the growth of real product should be accounted for by the growth of real factor inputs. Thus, the residual, which is the excess of the former over the latter, should be negligible if all measurements are correct.

In the aggregate production function an increase in total factor productivity (technical progress) is represented by a shift of that function, while increases in output caused by increases in inputs are represented by a move along the function. The theory underlying the work of Jorgenson and Griliches is that only *costless* changes cause shifts in the function, and these have to be separated from changes in output brought about by the use of scarce resources which have alternative uses. This separation involves obtaining reliable estimates of real output and of real factor input. Their contribution lies essentially in identifying real factor inputs by applying appropriate deflators to the income-streams going to factors. In doing so, they use the framework of social accounting: all prices are assumed to reflect private costs and benefits only, and only market transactions are included. Their method is as follows.

If Y_i and q_i are the quantity and price of the ith output, and X_j and p_j the quantity and price of the jth input, then we have the following identity:

$$\Sigma Y_i q_i = \Sigma X_j p_j \qquad (9)$$

Differentiating equation (9) with respect to time and dividing by the corresponding total value, we get:

$$\Sigma W_i \left\{ \frac{\dot{q}_i}{q_i} + \frac{\dot{Y}_i}{Y_i} \right\} = \Sigma V_j \left\{ \frac{\dot{p}_j}{p_j} + \frac{\dot{X}_j}{X_j} \right\} \qquad (10)$$

where W_i and V_j are the relative shares of the value of the ith output in total output, and of the jth input in total input, respectively.

[1] D. Jorgenson and Z. Griliches, 'The Explanation of Productivity Change', *Review of Economic Studies*, 1967.

Equation (10) is the identity between the weighted average of the sum of output prices and quantities and the weighted average of the sum of input prices and quantities.

From equation (10), the growth of the quantity of total output equals the weighted average growth of individual output quantities. Thus

$$\frac{\dot{Y}}{Y} = \Sigma W_i \frac{\dot{Y}_i}{Y_i} \tag{11}$$

Similarly for inputs

$$\frac{\dot{X}}{X} = \Sigma V_j \frac{\dot{X}_j}{X_j} \tag{12}$$

and similarly for the growth of output and input prices

$$\frac{\dot{q}}{q} = \Sigma W_i \frac{\dot{q}_i}{q_i} \tag{13}$$

$$\frac{\dot{p}}{p} = \Sigma V_j \frac{\dot{p}_j}{p_j} \tag{14}$$

These are Divisia quantity and price indexes. Total factor productivity (P) is the ratio of the quantity of output (Y) to the quantity of input (X):

$$P = \frac{Y}{X} \tag{15}$$

Using the Divisia indexes given above, the rate of growth of total factor productivity can be shown in two alternative ways:

$$\frac{\dot{P}}{P} = \frac{\dot{Y}}{Y} - \frac{\dot{X}}{X} = \Sigma W_i \frac{\dot{Y}_i}{Y_i} - \Sigma V_j \frac{\dot{X}_j}{X_j} \tag{16}$$

and

$$\frac{\dot{P}}{P} = \frac{\dot{p}}{p} - \frac{\dot{q}}{q} = \Sigma V_j \frac{\dot{p}_j}{p_j} - \Sigma W_i \frac{\dot{q}_i}{q_i} \tag{17}$$

The hypothesis of Jorgenson and Griliches is that the growth of total factor productivity is negligible. It must be emphasized that although the equality of inputs and outputs appears as an identity above, it is nevertheless a testable hypothesis as inputs and outputs are measured independently. Their method is to correct as many errors of measurement as possible. Their results are presented in a wealth of detail but may be summarized as in Table 11.2.

TABLE 11.2. *Rates of Growth of Output, Input, and Total Factor Productivity U.S.A., 1945–65*

	Output	Input	Productivity	(Input/ Output) (%)
1. Initial estimates	3·49	1·83	1·60	52·4
Estimates after correction for:				
2. Errors of aggregation	3·39	1·84	1·49	54·3
3. Errors in investment goods prices	3·59	2·19	1·41	61·0
4. Errors in relative utilization	3·59	2·57	0·96	71·6
5. Errors in aggregation of capital services	3·59	2·97	0·58	82·7
6. Errors in aggregation of labour services	3·59	3·47	0·10	96·7

Source: D. Jorgenson and Z. Griliches, *op. cit.*, Tables I–IX.

The first line in the table represents the results of the conventional calculation. Here growth of inputs can only account for just over one-half of the growth of output (U.S.A. private domestic product at constant prices).

The first correction is to allow for errors in aggregating output, labour and capital services at constant prices. Increases in these quantities are now measured using Divisia indexes. This slightly reduces the rate of growth of output and slightly increases the rate of growth of inputs (line 2).

The second adjustment corrects for errors in the measurement of investment goods prices. In the U.S.A. national accounts, the indexes of investment goods prices are largely based on input prices in these industries. The correct measure is output prices, which tend to grow more slowly, due (at least in part) to increased productivity in investment goods industries. Thus, a smaller price deflator is applied which increases the rate of growth of inputs. At this stage (line 3), inputs account for 61% of the growth of output.

Jorgensen and Griliches then drop the assumption (made in line 1) that the flow of factor (input) services is proportional to stocks of factors. They produce evidence that capital and, to a lesser extent, labour are being increasingly intensively utilized. The adjustment for

162

this error means that inputs now account for 71·6% of the growth of output.

Finally (lines 4 and 5), they correct for errors in the aggregation of capital and labour services. The net result is that, over the period, the rate of growth of inputs accounts for 96·7% of the growth of output. The residual has virtually disappeared. The increase in total factor productivity or technical progress is approximately zero.

This is not to say, of course, that advance in knowledge does not occur, but simply that the benefit accrues to those who incur the cost in bringing it about. In a sense, it is a matter of classification. If productivity increases, Jorgenson and Griliches impute this as an increase in factor inputs, while Denison treated it as a residual. Whether the sponsors are able to reap all the benefits of any increases in knowledge is an important question. For, if so, it follows that private and social rates of return to (for example) research and development expenditures are equal.

Inevitably, the authors have had to make a series of strong assumptions, but the results are nevertheless very interesting. They are especially so because Jorgenson and Griliches make all the usual neo-classical assumptions. Thus, three studies, each based on more or less the same conceptual framework, come up with three widely different estimates of technical progress; and the implication is that the precise meaning that can be given to these estimates of technical progress is not clear. The basic difficulty is that there is no clear definition of precisely what technical progress—or the residual, or advances in knowledge, or changes in total factor productivity—are. We are not likely to discover the quantitative importance of technological changes from these studies.

TECHNICAL PROGRESS FUNCTIONS, AND LEARNING BY DOING

In the work of Solow and Denison, technical progress is seen as being, in some sense, capable of substitution for inputs of capital and labour. That is to say, it is held to be possible to separate out the contributions of all of the various influences causing output to grow. In production function terms, these methods attempt to separate out shifts in the function from moves along the function. The possibility that the amount of investment in capital goods may influence the rate of technical progress is not allowed for, either in the models we have discussed or, for that matter, in models where technical progress has to be embodied in new capital equipment.

We propose to discuss models which regard technical progress in a rather different way. We deal with these briefly as they are models of the growth process, rather than attempts to measure technological

163

change. It should be apparent that we have not intended to survey either growth models or those growth models which incorporate technical progress.[1] We have, indeed, returned to talking of technical progress, rather than of technological change. We think it worth devoting some space to such approaches, because they further serve to indicate the complex ways in which technical progress is related to economic growth.

On one view, technical progress is part of a learning process.[2] Entrepreneurs do not have knowledge of the best techniques, and improvements in techniques come from familiarity with the problem involved. Learning is the product of experience. What variable are we to use as a proxy for experience? An obvious candidate is output. Learning occurs as a result of the repetition of the same activity—the higher the level of cumulative output, the greater the repetition, and the greater is learning. It appears that learning is subject to sharply diminishing returns. In a much-quoted case (the production of air-frames), the number of man-hours to produce an air-frame is a decreasing function of the number of the same sort of air-frame previously produced. It appears that the function is surprisingly precise and, in fact, to produce the nth frame of a given type, the labour required is proportional to $1/(3\sqrt{n})$.

Output appears to determine learning. However, if the rate of output were constant, then it would imply that the rate of learning is subject to diminishing returns. When output is constant, gross investment is positive. As machines are rarely replaced by precisely the same sort of machines, the environment in which production takes place changes, and the stimulus to learning changes. Thus, experience is better measured by cumulative investment. Arrow uses the integral of past gross investment as his index of experience.

Up to a point, a similar sort of approach to technical progress is followed by Kaldor.[3] Again, the relationship between investment and technical progress is made a two-way one. The ability of an economy to increase the amount of capital per man depends on its ability to innovate. Because increasing capital per man is held to entail the introduction of new techniques, most techniques come from inventive activity. On the other hand, most inventions require more capital per man. It follows from this that it is not possible to separate

[1] For two such surveys, see F. Hahn and R. Matthews, 'The Theory of Economic Growth: A Survey', *Economic Journal*, 1964; and C. Kennedy and A. Thirlwall, 'Technical Progress: A Survey', *Economic Journal*, 1972.

[2] K. Arrow, 'The Economic Implications of Learning by Doing', *Review of Economic Studies*, 1962.

[3] N. Kaldor, 'A Model of Economic Growth', *Economic Journal*, 1957; and N. Kaldor and J. Mirlees, 'A New Model of Economic Growth', *Review of Economic Studies*, 1961–62.

out increases in output due to invention and innovation (shifts in the production function) from those due to more capital per man (moves along the production function). Instead a technical progress function is proposed which relates the rate of growth in the productivity of labour working on new equipment to the rate of growth of investment per man.

At a constant rate of investment, there will be some increase in output per head, and thus the technical progress function has a positive intercept. The technical progress function exhibits 'diminishing returns'. The idea behind this is that the flow of *inventive ideas* is exogenous and constant. Increasing the rate of investment permits more ideas to be explored and applied: not all are equally productive and the implication is that those with the greatest potential are exploited first. The curve (see Fig. 11.2) thus reflects the 'technical

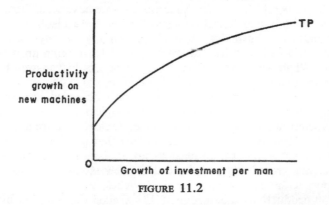

FIGURE 11.2

dynamism' of the economy, or the willingness to apply the flow of ideas which are themselves determined exogenously. An increase in the flow of ideas will shift the curve upwards, enabling any rate of growth of investment to lead to a more rapid rate of growth of labour productivity on new machines.

In both of these models there are external economies to investment. The investor receives less than his social marginal product, for the act of investment causes learning or technical progress—and the benefits of these do not entirely accrue to the investor. The result is that in studies such as Denison's the role of capital accumulation will tend to be understated, although, as we have seen, it is the view of Denison that this is simply a matter of classification. There is more to it than this, however. If the social returns to investment exceed the private returns, then, from a social point of view, too little investment will occur.

165

CONCLUSIONS

Measurements of technical progress, and of technological change, have thrown up rather confusing results. Basically, this is because of variations in the extent to which improvements in the quality of the factor inputs are included as increases in those inputs, or as technical progress. This is partly a matter of classification, but there is a very real conceptual problem. If an invention opens up profitable invest-ment opportunities, and the rate of investment increases as a result, then the rate of growth of output will rise. Is this increase in the rate of growth due to the invention, or to investment? Without the invention the increase in investment would not have occurred, whereas without the investment the invention would not have in-creased output. Models with embodied technical progress are able to cope with this dilemma to some extent, but by their nature pre-clude the answer to the original question. As we have seen, Denison's attempt to analyse technical progress further and to isolate the role of advances in knowledge—which are roughly synonymous with scientific and technological advance—did at least come up with an answer. When all is said and done, however, his answer is yet another residual.

An alternative approach to starting with observed growth and working back, to see what is due to technological advance, is to start with expenditure aimed at securing technological advance and move forwards. However, in Chapter 10 we saw that this latter approach was not very promising, at least as an explanation of differential productivity growth between industries. Few studies have followed this approach at an aggregate level. Griliches, as an extension of his work on productivity measurement, has argued that another bias in conventional total factor productivity measurements is the omission of the growth of research capital as a source of growth.[1] Research and development expenditures are likely to have their impact on output growth after long time lags, and some may have no identifi-able impact at all. Public expenditure will not contribute to measured productivity growth, unless it has external benefits, because (by convention) productivity growth in the public sector is zero. Thus, it is not clear which research and development expenditures should be included. After making a series of strong assumptions, Griliches calculates that the contribution of research and development ex-penditures to productivity growth in the U.S.A. has been about 0·06 percentage points—which is pretty small. This result is open, however, to the objections that we have referred to earlier. As it is

[1] Z. Griliches, 'Research Expenditures and Growth Accounting'. Paper read to the Conference of the International Economics Association, 1971.

very difficult to calculate the *ex post* returns to particular items of research or development expenditure, it is not particularly surprising that we have no generally accepted measure of the aggregate return.

In the chapters on innovation, we saw that to be successful an innovation required much more than technological expertise. Managerial skills were required to match marketing and production efforts with research activities. Investment is usually required to take advantage of the opportunities offered by technical change. Labour may have to adjust to new working conditions and acquire new skills. We also saw that the speed at which innovations are adopted by firms, and by consumers, will determine the extent to which innovations will increase output—both that part of the increase in output that is measured in the national accounts, and that part that is not. Thus, for scientific and technological advances to contribute to the growth of firms or industries requires the co-operation of a whole host of complementary influences, many of which have nothing to do with science or technology. It is our contention that a similar conclusion can be drawn when we consider the growth of national output. It is because of the existence of these complementary influences that it does not seem possible to isolate the role of science, technology, education, investment, or of any individual influence.

Epilogue

So far we have only touched tangentially on several matters which will strike many readers as being of paramount importance—not only because they concern the continued survival of life itself on this planet, but because they are central to their understanding of what economics is about.

If we attempted to draw up a balance-sheet of the contributions of science to civilization, we should have to put on one side discoveries like penicillin and, on the other, the unprecedented horror of modern warfare, pollution on a global scale, and the population explosion. In such circumstances, it may well be argued that to discuss science in relation to economic growth as though both were in the 'plus' category of human affairs is as laughable as it is unimaginative.

We think not, for the following reasons. First, the GNP is an index of output weighted by value. The weights can be altered to express different valuations of various components. If, for instance, cars are demoted, macrobiotic rice can be promoted, either by changes in market prices, or by a system of shadow pricing. More importantly, when pollution has to be controlled, the costs of controlling it can more easily be met out of a higher *total* output of goods and services, in the sense that less has to be given up to clear up the pollution. It follows, then, that the GNP is (in a deep sense) a neutral index of economic activity, independent of the good or bad consequences of that activity.

Further, the fact that we have spoken of economic growth throughout does not imply that our prime consideration is growth at all costs. It is not. Both of us might easily favour a lower level of output in certain circumstances (to achieve more equality, for example). But it must be said that where people have had a choice, they have tended over the years to choose higher rather than lower incomes, which implies changes in the direction of more output. The problem, in our view, is to design measures to control the adverse environmental consequences of economic change which are acceptable, feasible and compatible with other things that people want. This is a familiar economic problem; science merely gives it a more catastrophic tinge.

Lastly, we have argued that science has important economic consequences but that it must be regarded partly as part of society's creative, surging activity—an end, like art, rather than a means to further other ends. If the pursuit of this end has bad consequences, as well as good, it is up to society to say so, and to stop it. A nice calculus of less and more may help it to weigh matters up more justly.

INDEX